CONTENTS

SO-BBB-727

News
YOU CAN USE

TOPIC	SCRIPTURE	PAGE

News

YOU CAN USE

101 SERMON ILLUSTRATIONS

by **Mikal Keefer**

Loveland, Colorado

Group resources actually work!

This Group resource helps you focus on **"The 1 Thing"**—a life-changing relationship with Jesus Christ. "The 1 Thing" incorporates our **R.E.A.L.** approach to ministry. It reinforces a growing friendship with Jesus, encourages long-term learning, and results in life transformation, because it's:

Relational
Learner-to-learner interaction enhances learning and builds Christian friendships.

Experiential
What learners experience through discussion and action sticks with them up to 9 times longer than what they simply hear or read.

Applicable
The aim of Christian education is to equip learners to be both hearers and doers of God's Word.

Learner-based
Learners understand and retain more when the learning process takes into consideration how they learn best.

News You Can Use
101 Sermon Illustrations

Visit our Web site: **www.group.com**

Credits

Editor: Candace McMahan
Chief Creative Officer: Joani Schultz
Copy Editor: Amber Van Schooneveld
Art Director: Jean Bruns
Assistant Art Director: Joyce Douglas
Book Designer: Jenette McEntire

Print Production Artist: Jan Fonda
Illustrator: Matt Wood
Cover Art Director/Designer: Jeff A. Storm
Cover Photographer: Rodney Stewart
Production Manager: Peggy Naylor

Unless otherwise noted, Scripture taken from the HOLY BIBLE, NEW INTERNATIONAL VERSION®. Copyright © 1973, 1978, 1984 by International Bible Society. Used by permission of Zondervan Publishing House. All rights reserved.

Library of Congress Cataloging-in-Publication Data
Keefer, Mikal, 1954-
News you can use : 101 sermon illustrations / Mikal Keefer.
      p.   cm.
Includes indexes.
ISBN 0-7644-2935-3 (pbk. : alk. paper)
1. Homiletical illustrations. I. Title.
BV4225.3.K45 2005
251' .08--dc22

2005023775

10 9 8 7 6 5 4 3 2 1   15 14 13 12 11 10 09 08 07 06

Printed in the United States of America.

TOPIC	SCRIPTURE	PAGE

DEDICATION

To Bob, Tom, Kent,
    and all the other pastors
    who connect God's Word
    with real life.

Your sermons change the world.

INTRODUCTION

Welcome to *News You Can Use*

No matter how masterful a storyteller you are, your sermon illustrations just got more compelling.

That's because as you blend these 101 illustrations into your sermons, staff devotions, or workshops, you'll do *more* than just tell a great story.

True, these illustrations *are* great stories—and true ones, too. They're interest-grabbing gems handpicked from newspapers around the world. They're memorable—and crafted to complement your sermons and talks.

But these illustrations also pack a one-two wallop you won't find in other illustration books:

1. You get eye-catching *visual elements* for each illustration, professionally designed and ready for you to plug into PowerPoint and splash up on a screen behind you as you speak.

2. With every illustration you get the chance to engage your congregation in *instant application*. Your illustrations won't just entertain; they'll prompt life-changing interaction with your congregation!

Your presentation style is all your own—honed by experience and training. But every speaker needs illustrations, and these are tools you'll want in your sermon-preparation toolbox.

Use them as written, or adapt them to fit your style and situation. It's up to you. They're easily adapted, so you're in control.

However you use these illustrations to add salsa to your sermons, get ready to have some fun. They're more than just stories—they're *News You Can Use*.

News You Can Use: A User's Guide

You already know how to use sermon illustrations, but take a moment to read this section anyway. You'll discover how to wring every ounce of value from this book—and pack even more power into your sermons.

1. PLACE THESE ILLUSTRATIONS IN YOUR SERMON WHEREVER YOU WISH. Your sermons have a cadence, a rhythm that flows as you move from one point to the next. Often, illustrations provide transitions and breathing room while your congregation processes key points you've just shared.

Use these illustrations as transitions or to reinforce a point in your sermon—to hang a real-world example on principles and ideas you've just shared.

Or you might use an illustration to dive into a subject. News stories are excellent lead-ins to a sermon; people are accustomed to zeroing in on news stories and paying close attention.

These illustrations work anywhere in a sermon—just adapt as necessary.

2. YOU'LL NOTICE ILLUSTRATIONS ARE WRITTEN IN A CONVERSATIONAL STYLE. However you use these illustrations, it's easy to adapt the conversational text leading into and out of the illustrations to match your own voice. Simply change the wording to fit your sermon, situation, and style.

Or just use the illustrations as written—they'll preach!

3. USE THE VISUALS WE'VE PROVIDED. Each illustration comes with both a headline slide and a second visual you can project on a screen as you share the story. We've also included a neutral background slide to use as a transition between the headline and photo or anywhere else during the sermon. Using a visual element snags the attention of visual learners—and, according to Penn State's Institute for the Study of Adult Literacy, that's about 65 percent of your congregation.

The images are in PowerPoint format, so to project them you'll need a computer and a projection system connected to it. Visit www.microsoft .com/downloads for information about downloads for both PC and Macintosh platforms. Or an even quicker solution is to wander into the next youth group meeting and ask if any of the teenagers have suggestions about how to set up your program.

4. CONSIDER CITING SOURCES. Quickly mentioning an illustration's source packs power into the story. It lets your congregation know these aren't lifted-off-the-Internet urban legends. Rather, these illustrations have been professionally published by legitimate news agencies in credible papers. They're fact, not fiction.

You aren't *required* to mention a source, but you'll see your congregation perk up when you lead into an illustration by saying, "According to the Detroit Free Press..." or "The Associated Press reported that..."

Some of your congregation will be impressed that you've tracked down a true story to illustrate your point. The rest will be stunned that you're so widely read!

5. FEEL FREE TO USE THESE ILLUSTRATIONS AS YOU SEE FIT. We suggest topics we think connect well with each illustration, but you may see another way to use a story. That's fine. Let your creativity and inspiration be your guide.

6. CONSIDER USING THE ILLUSTRATION APPLICATION PROVIDED WITH EACH STORY. With each illustration you get a suggestion for incorporating an action step. That step may be a quick discussion between congregation members, writing something in the church bulletin or on an index card, or taking a vote. On pages 10-14, you'll find a complete explanation of all six options—they're worth taking a look.

Remember: *You use illustrations to engage your listeners and help them more deeply connect with the point you're making in your message.* Turbocharging your illustration by having congregation members respond to it will make the point of your message that much *more* memorable—and cement that much more learning.

You know your congregation and church culture best, but don't be afraid to stretch your congregation now and then with an Illustration Application. It'll keep your congregation on its toes!

7. HAVE FUN. The majority of these illustrations can easily be delivered in a way that makes them funny or whimsical. Have fun with them, dropping them into your messages when it's time to change your pacing, reduce tension, or move to a serious point.

A Quick Word About "True" Illustrations

Every effort has been made to source these illustrations so you can share them with confidence. We've tracked down printed sources and reliable Web sites and checked these illustrations against collections of urban legends to ensure nothing untrue sneaks through.

But that doesn't mean we haven't been hoodwinked.

It happens…as the following story demonstrates.

A Christian author received a call a few years ago that snagged his attention: *The Tonight Show* was on the line, asking that he call back to chat with Jay Leno.

For an author, a guest shot on *The Tonight Show* is a big deal. A *huge* deal. It can launch a book faster than shooting that book out of a rocket.

The author phoned Leno, unsure what to expect but delighted to be talking with *The Tonight Show* host.

Leno wanted to chat about the author's latest book, but not to praise it. Rather, Leno had a problem with a specific story in the book.

The author had mentioned Leno's classic car collection and described how much Leno spent to acquire a motorcycle once owned by Elvis Presley. The amount was staggering and had been reported in newspapers and at least one other book.

The problem: It never happened.

Leno wasn't sure how the rumor started, but he *was* sure he wanted it to go away. Fast. The rumor portrayed him as a Hollywood star with money to burn—an image he didn't appreciate.

Members of Leno's staff had tracked down every printed or broadcast reference to the Presley motorcycle story they could find, and Leno was personally following up to get the story out of print and off the air.

Ouch.

The author had done his homework. He'd found reliable sources. But still…there he was on the phone with Leno, who politely suggested the story immediately be taken out of print.

We hope to not receive phone calls from any plucked geese, Japanese pizza makers, Jerusalem post office clerks, or other personalities who appear in the following illustrations.

But if a false story *has* somehow made it into these pages, let us know. We'll do what our author friend did: remove the story when the book is reprinted.

And just in case Jay Leno's staff is reading—we never believed that motorcycle story in the first place.

And we're available for an interview.

Call us anytime.

Illustration Applications

Your congregation has just heard a great story…but so what?

Perhaps you shared the illustration, and that's enough. It accomplished its purpose, and the pacing of your message requires you to move along.

But if you'd like to pause for a few moments and extend the experience, following are six ways you can easily do so. We recommend one of the following applications for each illustration, but with a bit of creativity you can use any of these with any illustration.

 **DISCUSSION**

Prompt a Discussion

If you want to involve your congregation, give people a chance to talk. And not just some people—include *everyone*.

An easy way to do this is to ask people to turn to a neighbor and answer a question or two that you suggest from the pulpit. We recommend questions that don't require a great deal of transparency because you don't know if people are sitting next to friends or strangers.

If you launch discussions, have with you an audio signal of some sort that will refocus attention on yourself when the allotted time for discussion has passed. A referee's whistle is too shrill and abrupt, and a whisper too subdued. Consider using a tinkling bell (no gongs!) or a mellow-toned wooden whistle.

Let the people in your congregation know how long they'll have to talk (a minute or two is usually plenty), and give a 30-second and 15-second countdown warning so participants can wrap up their conversations gracefully.

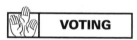 **VOTING**

Take a Vote

When you ask congregation members to raise their hands in response to a question, you force a decision—and involvement.

A simple show of hands is enough, though you can let people vote in other ways. For instance, as people enter the sanctuary, you might distribute a dollar bill to each and then have them vote during the offering by designating each returned dollar bill as a "yes" vote and each kept dollar bill a "no" vote. That would be an interesting spin for a stewardship message!

Affirming one answer or another with applause or by calling out a word is another option. Standing up works, too, though it's important to be sensitive to congregation members who can't stand.

 **SOUVENIR**

Pass Out Souvenirs

Now and then give each congregation member something he or she can take home as a reminder of your message.

Souvenirs don't have to be expensive. A four-cent washer from the hardware store can be a reminder of the need for a centered, balanced life. (You'll point out that the hole in the washer is in the precise center of the metal disk and lets you balance it evenly on a fingertip.) A pencil eraser makes a great reminder of God's grace and forgiveness. A fancy paper clip can remind listeners of the need to stay connected to each other—and to God.

The best sources of inexpensive souvenirs are hardware stores, grocery stores, and office-supply stores—anywhere items are sold inexpensively and in bulk. And while most vacation souvenirs are exotic reminders of a place, everyday items connect spiritual truth to objects your congregation is likely to see often.

 **INTERVIEW**

Conduct an Interview

This isn't a technique for the fainthearted, but it quickly generates interest. Leave the stage, and wander down an aisle with a microphone in hand to find out what a few congregation members thought about the illustration you just shared. A few carefully framed questions will help the people you interview connect the point of your message with the illustration…and expand on it for you.

The danger is interviewing someone who wasn't listening or who is terrified of the microphone. You won't want to put anyone on the spot, so ask for volunteers—and choose carefully!

A safer interview solution: Ask congregation members *before* your message to serve on a panel. Prep them with the questions you'll ask, and share any timing expectations you have.

Two tips about conducting interviews:

1. NEVER SURRENDER THE MICROPHONE. As long as you're holding the microphone, *you* control how long someone talks, and you can quickly remove the microphone if an answer starts wandering.

Many people are uncomfortable using microphones. A microphone at waist level won't be helpful. If you're holding the microphone, you can place it where it will pick up the speaker's voice.

2. KEEP IT BRIEF. You may well have more interview than you have time. Don't be afraid to say, "We have time for one more comment" and then move on. It's better to leave a congregation wanting more than wishing you'd stopped earlier.

And count on people you've told to take one minute to take at least two, even if they've rehearsed their answers. It's just human nature, so factor in extra time.

 **WRITING**

Put It in Writing

Sometimes we suggest that members of your congregation respond to an illustration by writing something they can tuck away and read later. You can provide index cards as people enter the room, or if your church distributes bulletins, leave room for a written response on a specific page you can point out to your congregation.

If congregation members won't be asked to share what they wrote, say so. It will allow for more open, honest writing.

 **ACTIVITY**

Do It Now

If you want members of your congregation to apply what they've learned, why not give them a chance right on the spot? Consider taking a two-minute break to let people actually get up and do something.

Please note that the *last* thing some people want at church is to interact with others; either through culture or inclination, they're accustomed to quietly shuffling in and then quietly shuffling out.

When you ask for action, you invade some peoples' personal space...and they'll let you know about it. But perhaps that's the best thing that could happen.

This technique for turbocharging your illustrations (and sermons) isn't appropriate in every instance, but it *is* an option to consider.

Two factors to keep in mind as you wander into the minefield of actually asking your congregation to *do* something:

1. RESPECT CULTURE. If nobody has had to respond immediately to a sermon preached in your church for the past 50 years, it's probably wise to start with a less intrusive illustration application before diving into an activity application.

2. RESPECT ARCHITECTURE. If your congregation is packed into pews, getting people up and moving around might be difficult logistically. Scale the requests you make for action to fit your church's architecture.

Take a Risk

If application matters to you, be aware that the longer the time between hearing a truth and acting on it, the less likely your congregation will do anything about that truth.

Jesus was a *big* fan of requiring quick action once someone had been exposed to truth. Follow *now*. Repent *now*. Embrace a new life *now*.

We'd be wise to take a cue from the master Teacher.

You know your congregation and church culture, so you know what you can get away with. What will prompt a response. How far and fast to push as you seek to make messages memorable, and truth applicable.

What's safe is to never push the envelope at all…but "safe" messages are seldom life-changing ones.

World's Oldest Wine in a Barrel

TOPIC: Aging
SCRIPTURE: Proverbs 20:29

Ever heard that people, like fine wine, mellow with age?

That theory—about wine, at least—was put to the test in Strasbourg, France, when officials sniffed and tasted what's reported to be the world's oldest wine in a barrel. It's a barrel of white wine that's been aging for more than 500 years.

POWERPOINT SHOW: Aging

The 1472 vintage wine has an alcohol content of 9.4 percent, and to offset evaporation, one bottle of dry white wine is added to the barrel four times per year.

But make no mistake: In spite of evaporation, the composition of the wine confirms it's a 1472 vintage.

And it's worth noting that, at least for this barrel, the wine didn't mellow with age. Instead, it has become highly acidic.

Let's hope the same can't be said about us as *we* get older.

 **INTERVIEW**

Unless your church is very unusual, it has a few gray-haired people in the congregation. Briefly interview an appropriate person by asking:

• **What are the benefits of getting older?**

• **In what ways has growing older affected your relationship with God?**

• **What advice would you have for a young person in the congregation?**

Contact your interview subject before the service to confirm he or she will be in attendance and to share the questions you'll be asking.

SOURCE: Agence France-Presse, "After 531 Years, World's Oldest Wine in a Barrel Still Has Fine Aroma"

Great Britain: Land of Crumpets and Crumpled Fenders

TOPIC: Anger
SCRIPTURE: James 1:19-20

POWERPOINT SHOW: Anger

When you think about the British, what image comes to mind?

Polite tea parties and gentlemanly games of cricket? Long hikes in the quiet countryside?

Well, think again.

According to a national survey backed by the RAC Foundation and published in the Max Power car magazine, 80.4 percent of United Kingdom drivers report they've been the victims of road rage. Some 70 percent confess they've *committed* road-rage offenses, though only 14 percent indicate any remorse for their actions.

An earlier survey published by the RAC Foundation concluded that 600,000 British drivers have been physically attacked in road-rage incidents. More than a million drivers have been rammed by another motorist.

And we thought people got angry around *here*.

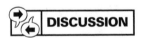 **DISCUSSION**

Do this: Quickly turn to someone sitting near you and answer this question:

- **What's the one thing that most quickly angers you when you encounter it in another driver?**

Maybe it's changing lanes without signaling or driving while on a cell phone. Whatever it is, share it with a neighbor in the next 30 seconds.

SOURCE: The Scotsman, "Britain Has Highest Road-Rage Rate in Europe" by Dan McDougall

School Board Votes Easy to Count

TOPIC: Apathy
SCRIPTURE: Hebrews 10:24

It's one thing to run for office and lose. It happens all the time.

But it's another thing to run unopposed and *still* lose.

That's what happened to Carl Miner of Blytheville, Arkansas, when he ran unopposed for a seat on the South Mississippi County School Board. Nobody voted for him. Nobody. Not even *Miner* voted for himself—he

POWERPOINT SHOW: Apathy

went to a polling place, but it was closed when he arrived.

Officials say it was the first time in the history of Mississippi County that nobody in the entire precinct voted for a candidate.

And Miner? Despite running unopposed, he was denied the school board seat because nobody in his precinct voted for him.

It's true: You can't win for losing.

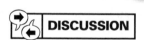 **DISCUSSION**

Maybe you're one of those folks who don't get involved in the political process because you don't think your vote could make a difference.

Carl Miner could tell you otherwise. If anyone had voted for him—and I mean *anyone*—he'd have won a seat on the school board.

Turn to someone near you and discuss this question:

• **When did one person's involvement in your life make a huge difference?**

Maybe someone jumped to your defense in an argument; or someone told the truth, and that validated you; or someone loved you and changed your life.

Briefly share that story with someone now.

SOURCE: WorldNow and KPOM, "Man Fails in Uncontested School Board Race"

Winkle Gets New Tombstone

TOPIC: Appearances
SCRIPTURE: Jeremiah 17:10

POWERPOINT SHOW: Appearances

When a stonemason in southwestern England found an old limestone carving in a quarry, he carried it home. The stone ended up out in his yard, serving as a tombstone for Winkle, the stonemason's cat.

An amateur historian noticed the carving and suggested that it might, in fact, be not just an old carving. It might be a *very* old carving.

The 1,000-year-old carving, dating from the ninth or 10th century, has now been sold at auction for more than $465,000 (Canadian).

And Winkle? Winkle has apparently had to get accustomed to a new tombstone.

ACTIVITY

If you're like me, you sometimes misjudge things when you're considering only appearances. Maybe you've met someone who was attractive but deeply flawed. Perhaps you've walked through an art gallery and found yourself wondering why anyone would pay money for some of the paintings you saw there.

Appearances can be deceiving.

And that's why I'm glad God looks beneath the surface at the heart.

I'm going to ask you to stand now and do this: Turn slowly in a complete circle. Look at the people God has brought together in this room. Ask God to allow you to see this collection of people through his eyes. See them as God's sons and daughters, as children of God.

SOURCE: The Associated Press, "Carving Found in Rural British Garden Fetches Small Fortune at Auction"

Illinois Potluck Police Stand Down

TOPIC: Authority
SCRIPTURE: Romans 13:1-3

In the church, we hear a *lot* about authority…

Pay Caesar what he's owed.

Do your work as if you're working for the Lord.

And at least in Illinois, be sure the meatloaf you bring to the church potluck is thoroughly cooked so the health inspector doesn't get upset.

Wait…scratch that last item. The authority of local health inspectors no longer extends to Illinois church potlucks.

The Illinois governor has declared that as long as the potlucks don't charge fees and don't happen on public property, churches can serve potentially hazardous potato salad to their hearts' delight.

In the past, laws governing public health were sufficiently vague that more than one church potluck was shut down by health inspectors.

So bring on the Jell-O salad and broccoli-cheese casseroles. They're legal now, even if they're *still* a bad idea.

POWERPOINT SHOW:
Authority

SOURCE: The Associated Press, "Church Potlucks Are Once Again Safe From Big Brother"

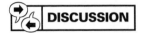 **DISCUSSION**

Anyone who's concerned about the authority of the government would probably consider regulation of church potlucks excessive. Anyone who appreciates not getting food poisoning might appreciate setting standards for food served anywhere—church basements included.

That's the thing about authority in our lives: It often limits our options, but it also often provides needed guidelines. It may not always be welcome, but it's often helpful.

Do this: Turn to someone sitting near you, and describe a time you dealt with authority and it didn't feel good at the time but turned out to be a good thing in the end.

Maybe it was getting an expensive traffic ticket that changed your driving habits for the better. Or maybe you wired your basement and hated having to do the job up to code, but now you realize your home is safer for it.

Share with your neighbor your story of dealing with authority.

Motivated Student Learns if at First You Don't Succeed...

TOPIC: Bible
SCRIPTURE: 2 Timothy 3:16-17

How much do *you* want to read the Bible?

Most of us have one or more Bibles in our homes. We have the time to read. We've got plenty of opportunities.

What we're missing is the motivation.

That's not a problem for a Cameroonian who just received his "First School Leaving Certificate," the award given when students pass their primary school exam.

What makes the award recipient, Atangana, stand out from his primary classmates is his age.

Atangana is 75 years old.

He dropped out of school in 1940 and returned to class, in part, so he could learn to read and write. And what reading material was so compelling that he was willing to sit in class with students the age of his friends' grandkids?

The Bible.

After six decades, Atangana decided he wanted to better understand God's Word— and that could happen best if he was able to read it himself.

POWERPOINT SHOW:
Bible

SOURCE: Reuters, "Man Passes Primary School Exam at 75"

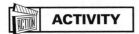 **ACTIVITY**

Do this: If you've brought a Bible, turn to a favorite passage—just one or two verses that have had meaning in your life. Don't have a Bible? Use a pew Bible [if there are some], or rely on your memory.

Got that passage fixed in your mind? On the count of three, we're all going to stand and read or recite—together and out loud—a few lines of a favorite passage. Don't worry if you get it word-for-word perfect; the point isn't to win a prize for memorization or reading. The point is to let some of what we've hidden in our hearts emerge through our mouths.

Ready? One…two…three.

For Malaysian Teachers Timing Is Everything

TOPIC: Busyness
SCRIPTURE: Ephesians 5:15-17

 VOTING

Has anyone here been too busy lately? Raise your hand if you think you're too busy. Now raise your hand if you're not busy enough.

You too-busy people: Check out who has their hands up, and see if you can give them some of your stuff that's not getting done.

How do you know when you're too busy?

Here's one sign: Your boss tells you that if you're going to have a baby, at least do it while you're on vacation.

That's the message female Malaysian teachers received from Malaysia's deputy education minister, Abdul Aziz Samsuddin.

POWERPOINT SHOW: Busyness

The minister stressed that the education ministry is *not* suggesting teachers stop reproducing. Clearly that would be bad for anyone in the business of educating children.

Rather, the education ministry wants teachers who have babies to coordinate conceptions and deliveries so not too many teachers are out of class at one time. Schools are busy places, and having too few staff on hand creates problems.

Maybe it's just me, but I'm thinking that the education minister's recommendation isn't going to catch on. If he thinks *schools* are busy places, he should see what it's like around a house where there's a new baby!

SOURCE: Japan Today, " 'Have Your Babies on Holidays' Teachers Told"

Singer Scores #1 Hits…Again

TOPIC: Career
SCRIPTURE: Proverbs 14:23

POWERPOINT SHOW: Career

It was a great week for Elvis Presley on the British singles chart. "Jailhouse Rock" was in the number one slot just days before, and then his hit "One Night" took top honors.

But in spite of the accomplishment, Elvis wasn't popping champagne corks back at Graceland. Why?

Because Elvis had been dead for more than 27 years.

To celebrate what would have been Elvis' 70th birthday, his record label re-released all 18 of Elvis' songs that hit number one in Britain. And so far, the tunes are hitting number one again.

Despite the fact Elvis is no longer alive, his career has never been hotter in Britain.

Anyone else think a career that allows you to make a fortune 27 years after you've died is worth considering? I'll sign up!

Of course, Elvis may be *enjoying* this part of his career less than when he was alive. Money clearly isn't everything.

 **DISCUSSION**

Turn to someone sitting near you, and answer this question:

• **Would you rather have a career you enjoy or a career that pays lots of money?**

Maybe you're blessed with an enjoyable career that also pays well, but if you had to choose—which would it be?

SOURCE: Agence France-Presse, "Elvis Tops British Singles Charts for Second Week Running"

Only Good News Need Apply

TOPIC: Christmas
SCRIPTURE: Luke 2:9-11

The German daily paper Bild took a novel approach to reporting news on Christmas Day: Only good news was allowed in the edition.

Rather than focusing on holiday traffic snarls, it applauded the fact that on Christmas no traffic wardens were working in Germany, and therefore no parking tickets would be issued.

POWERPOINT SHOW: Christmas 1

Instead of criticizing a politician who had just resigned because he accepted payment from a former employer while in office, the politician was congratulated on his government severance package.

Whether it was local, national, or international news, the slant was the same: relentlessly positive. For one day only, the 12 million readers of Bild received what's so rarely found in newspapers: good news.

Christmas is all about good news. Good news that a Savior has come, that a full manger in Bethlehem led to an empty tomb outside Jerusalem, and that we can be rescued from sin.

I have good news for you today—and his name is Jesus.

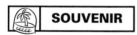 **SOUVENIR**

Before your congregation arrives, place a page from your local newspaper on each seat. This is a quiet way to distribute the newspaper, and it forces everyone to interact with it. An alternative: Distribute pages as people enter the room.

After you share this illustration, remind people of the newspaper they received, and ask that they read it later, looking for good news.

SOURCE: Reuters, "German Paper Prints Only Good News on Xmas"

This Time There's Room in the Inn

TOPIC: Christmas
SCRIPTURE: Luke 2:6-7

When it comes to a traditional Christmas pageant, it's the innkeeper who gets all the dirty looks.

What sort of person refuses to make room for a pregnant woman and demands that she deliver her baby in a stable? That Bethlehem innkeeper has damaged the reputation of innkeepers everywhere for 2,000 years.

So the Travelodge hotel in London's Covent Garden has decided to rectify the situation. Any couple can have a free night's stay on Christmas Eve…as long as their names are Mary and Joseph and they have identification to prove it.

So if you're part of a Mary and Joseph combo, plan your trip to London now.

But you might want to call in advance for a reservation. If too *many* namesake couples respond, there might not be—yet again—enough room in the inn.

Maybe we can find room in our hearts to forgive that unnamed innkeeper for his mistake. After all, he didn't know that Jesus was the Messiah.

But we do.

This Christmas season—every season—we face the same question the innkeeper faced: Will we make room for Jesus?

POWERPOINT SHOW:
Christmas 2

SOURCE: Reuters, "Plenty of Room at Inn for Mary and Joseph"

 **SOUVENIR**

Distribute key blanks to each person, and ask people to hold their keys as you lead them in prayer. Ask forgiveness for not always making room for Jesus in daily life and decisions. Ask for faithful hearts. Celebrate God's love shown through Jesus' birth in Bethlehem.

Encourage people to slide the blank keys onto their key chains so when they see them, they're reminded to make room for Jesus.

Note: To get key blanks, contact a local locksmith or hardware store early, and ask to buy them in bulk. Offer to take whatever old blanks are gathering dust in a bottom drawer and to buy the least expensive blanks available.

Packers vs. Jesus

TOPIC: Church
SCRIPTURE: Hebrews 10:24-25

POWERPOINT SHOW: Church

The St. Bernard Catholic Church in Green Bay, Wisconsin faced a tough situation.

The Green Bay Packers were playing at 2:00 p.m. on Christmas Eve. Mass was scheduled at 4:00 p.m.—earlier than the game would be over.

What to do in a town where Packer football is itself an unofficial religion?

It took some debate, but in the end, the pastor of St. Bernard didn't want parishioners to have to choose between coming to church and catching the Packers on television. Truth be told, some were a bit concerned how mass would fare if it came down to a choice.

So the two 4:00 p.m. Masses on Christmas Eve were cancelled, and an additional 6:00 p.m. Mass was scheduled instead.

Some parishioners were horrified that a church service would be changed to accommodate a football game. Other parishioners didn't see any problem. As long as they were able to go to church, why would it matter *when* they attended?

Assuming that the [name of a local team] ever make it to the playoffs, how would we respond? Is there something sacred about when we meet on Sundays?

Or is church about something else?

   **INTERVIEW**

Before your meeting, recruit three respected members of your congregation to interview. Ask:

- **Have you ever missed church because you were doing something else?**

- **What's important enough that you'd miss church to do it?**

Contact your interview subjects earlier to confirm they'll be in attendance and to share the questions you'll be asking.

SOURCE: The Associated Press, "Packers-Vikings Game Leads Churches to Change Services"

Wait...Wrong Address

TOPIC: Commitment
SCRIPTURE: Philippians 3:4-8

Political protester Jody Mason wanted to make a statement about war and the president's policies.

So Mason padlocked himself to the door of a building in Olympia, Washington—a building housing government offices and officials, a place where his committed voice of dissent would be heard.

POWERPOINT SHOW: Commitment

At least, that's what *might* have happened—if Mason had picked the right building.

Unfortunately, he chained himself to the Washington State Grange building instead of the U.S. Department of Energy building he'd targeted. The Grange is a nonprofit advocacy group that focuses on improving the lives of citizens who live in rural areas.

Mason had been chained to the door for 18 hours before Grange staff members told him he had the wrong address.

 **DISCUSSION**

You've got to give Mason credit: He was committed to his cause.
Here's a question to talk over with someone seated near you:
• **What's a cause for which *you'd* chain yourself to a door?**

Turn to someone near you and answer that question. You'll have two minutes to talk.

SOURCE: The Olympian, "Protester Gets Right Building"

Wait Until They Try to Plan a Vacation

TOPIC: Communication
SCRIPTURE: Matthew 6:3

POWERPOINT SHOW: Communication

Sometimes you can just tell that a couple is going to have communication issues when they marry. There are subtle signs, little signals.

And sometimes there are red, flashing neon lights spelling out "It's Time to Talk."

Ian Johnstone and Amy Dolby were dating in Britain when Ian decided to spend a year traveling around Australia. The 27-year-old bricklayer was already in Australia when he realized just how much he missed Amy.

So Ian earned enough money to take a flight home, surprise Amy, and ask for her hand in marriage.

Except she wasn't there. It turns out Amy had been missing Ian, too. So she had decided to surprise *him.*

They managed to miss each other as they each flew 11,000 miles in opposite directions. At one point they were in the same Singapore airport at the same time waiting for connecting flights, but they didn't see each other.

Ian proposed by phone in Britain when Amy contacted him from Australia. She accepted.

 **ACTIVITY**

All's well that ends well, right? Ian and Amy got together, and I got a great story to share with you about the importance of communication.

Let's apply that lesson. In a moment I'm going to ask you to get up and connect with someone here in the room long enough to share something important with that person. If you're married to him or her, it might be a simple "I love you." If you don't know the person, it might be a simple—but very important—"*Jesus* loves you."

Ready? Go.

SOURCE: Reuters, "Lovers Criss-Cross World in Vain"

Pooches From Heaven

TOPIC: Compassion
SCRIPTURE: Colossians 3:12

There are many definitions of compassion, but they all have one thing in common: Compassion requires that someone gets *involved*.

POWERPOINT SHOW: Compassion

Compassionate people usually don't have to ponder if they'll step up to help when help is needed. They've already made that decision. They're ready for action.

Just ask Gary Gallien of Florence, Alabama.

Gallien was working at an apartment complex when he decided to step outside. As he cleared the doorway, he heard a woman's scream, looked up, and saw an object hurtling toward him.

A white object.

A white, *furry* object.

Gallien stuck out his arms and caught the object, which turned out to be…a dog.

The pooch had clearly made a poor decision several floors up about catching a bird or experimenting with flight. Had Gallien not responded automatically and made the catch of his lifetime, that pooch would have been one dead dog.

 **SOUVENIR**

As a reminder of Gallien's compassion, I'm going to see that each of you gets something to take home with you: a dog biscuit.

Now, this biscuit isn't for you *personally*. Your job is to give it away to a pooch in your life—your dog, a neighbor's dog, a dog that's just passing by. Any dog that looks hungry and as if your compassion would make its day.

SOURCE: The Associated Press, "Man Catches Pooch That Fell From Balcony"

A Free Toaster Won't Fix *This*

TOPIC: Confession
SCRIPTURE: 1 John 1:8-10

POWERPOINT SHOW: Confession

Dozens of customers of the Kowloon branch of the Singapore-based DBS Bank got an unexpected call from the bank recently.

It was a confession.

During a renovation, the bank pulled some 920 safe-deposit boxes out of the vault and sent them to a scrap yard. Unfortunately, nobody checked to confirm that all of the boxes were, in fact, empty.

Eighty-three weren't.

The bank was able to reach most of the 83 customers by phone, but some of them first heard about the problem from a television news program.

Happily, some safe-deposit box contents were found at the scrap yard, so at least a few customers were able to retrieve their valuables.

But the other customers? Here's hoping the bank's confession will soothe tempers.

 **DISCUSSION**

OK, maybe the phone call might make things a *little* better.

But no apology is going to bring back Aunt Edna's brooch that you tucked away in the vault for your kids to inherit someday. Words just aren't going to cut it—or will they?

In a moment I'm going to ask you to turn to a neighbor and tell about a time that an apology and admission of guilt—one you received or one you offered—*did* matter.

The question again: **When has an apology and admission of guilt mattered in your life?**

Ready? You and your partner will both have about a minute to talk. Go.

SOURCE: FOX News, "Bank Boo-Boo Destroys Safe-Deposit Boxes"

Last Call Really *Is* Last Call

TOPIC: Conflict
SCRIPTURE: Ephesians 4:26

When Robert Tyrrell asked the staff of a village pub to serve him a drink, it was hardly something out of the ordinary. People had been ordering pints in the North Star Inn in Steventon, England, for generations. Since the 1500s to be exact.

POWERPOINT SHOW: Conflict

Besides, Tyrrell owned the pub, and he was giving a direct order to his employees.

Unfortunately, because it was after hours, the staff couldn't legally do Tyrrell's bidding. And *that* set up a conflict.

If you were Tyrrell, how would you have handled this situation?

 **INTERVIEW**

Let's do a bit of investigation, right here. How *would* you handle this conflict? I'm looking for a few volunteers who'll suggest some options.

If possible, walk from the platform or from behind the podium into the congregation while asking for volunteers. After prompting and repeating several answers, continue with the story.

Well, although it's an obvious solution, nobody suggested doing what Tyrrell actually did: He went outside, climbed into a bulldozer, and drove the bulldozer through the wall of his own pub.

Later, a more calm Tyrrell had the opportunity to ponder his conflict-resolution skills as he stood in the Oxford Crown Court.

Tyrrell pled guilty to the charge of causing criminal damage with reckless disregard for the lives of the employees who were inside the pub. That was bad enough.

But then there was also the issue of repairs, which were estimated to cost up to $112,000.

SOURCE: The Associated Press, "Man Bulldozes British Pub After Refused a Drink"

Confession Soothes Student's Conscience

TOPIC: Conscience
SCRIPTURE: Romans 13:4-5

POWERPOINT SHOW: Conscience

When a student in Colorado's Eagle County High School cheated on a Shakespeare test, she felt guilty...and rightly so.

The student stole the answers to the test, passed the exam, graduated, moved out of state, and went on with her life...sort of.

The principal of the school where the incident occurred has received a written confession from the student—47 years after the cheating incident.

The student is now a 65-year-old grandmother of five, and at long last she's soothed her conscience by confessing what she did.

The principal, Mark Strakbein, didn't revoke the woman's diploma. But he did read her letter—a heartfelt confession admitting her guilt—to every homeroom in the school.

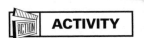 **ACTIVITY**

Don't worry—I'm not going to ask that we all turn to a neighbor and confess a wrong we did years ago.

But confession is important, in part because our conscience prompts us to put right whatever we can put right...and to ask forgiveness. And if we let God speak to all our hearts, few of us have consciences that are completely clear before him.

Let's do this: If there's something you've done that you want to be forgiven for or if it's been a challenge for you to forgive someone, join me as I stand. Just stand where you are while we pray as a community for God's grace *in* our lives and *through* our lives.

SOURCE: The Associated Press, "Grandmother Confesses to Cheating in 1957"

Speeding Ticket Proves Pricey

TOPIC: Consequences
SCRIPTURE: Jeremiah 4:18

First, let me say that I know nobody here has ever received a ticket for speeding.

But if you *were* to receive one—if you were ticketed for driving 46.5 mph in a 30-mph zone—how large a fine would you expect to pay?

POWERPOINT SHOW: Consequences

 VOTING

Raise your hand if you think $25 would be fair.
Fifty dollars?
Seventy-five dollars?
One hundred and fifty dollars?
How about $103,000?

That's the fine slapped on Finnish businessman Anssi Vanjoki for driving 16.5 miles above the limit.

In Finland traffic fines are linked to income, and since Vanjoki is a Nokia senior executive with a multimillion-dollar annual income, he was fined accordingly.

But don't rush to write a check to help him pay. Some Finnish Parliament members who want the law amended weighed in, and a court reduced Vanjoki's fine to $5,245…or a mere $317.87 for each mile he drove above the speed limit.

SOURCE: The Associated Press, "Finnish Man Gets Six-Figure Speeding Ticket" by Matti Huuhtanen

Happy Homeowner Refuses to Move

TOPIC: Contentment
SCRIPTURE: Philippians 4:11b-12

POWERPOINT SHOW: Contentment

How much do you love *your* house or apartment?

However much it is, there's a London pensioner who liked his more.

The two-bedroom London apartment that was the pensioner's home until he died is available for sale—with one stipulation.

If you buy the apartment—and it may be a good deal for $728,000—you're going to have a built-in roommate. That's because the former occupant isn't about to move out.

His ashes are in an urn on the fireplace mantle, and it's a term of sale that they must stay there.

 **INTERVIEW**

Before your meeting, recruit several members of your congregation to interview. Ask:

- **What in your life are you thoroughly content with?**

- **In what ways does being content affect your life? Is that for the better or for the worse?**

Contact your interview subjects earlier to confirm they'll be in attendance and to share the questions you'll be asking.

SOURCE: Reuters, "Apartment for Sale: Dead Owner's Ashes Included"

Italians Now Officially Able to Call Each Other #%^*@#$

TOPIC: Culture
SCRIPTURE: Romans 12:2

When in Rome, do as the Romans do.

That's the advice tour guides sometimes give, encouraging visitors to dive into the cultures they visit.

And now visitors can call out vulgarities as they dive because some crude language is officially sanctioned in Italy.

POWERPOINT SHOW: Culture

Italy's highest appeals court has ruled that from now on, vulgar language regarding body parts is an acceptable part of Italian culture. Vulgar language has become so much a part of everyday life that it no longer violates penal code article 594, which details "Crimes of Honor."

In days gone by, what now passes for heated but acceptable conversation sparked duels. *Legal* duels.

So if you're pulling into a parking spot in Rome and someone cuts you off, do as the Romans do. Don't reach for your dueling pistols. Instead, fire up your vocabulary.

That's not very good advice, is it?

The fact is that, as Christians, we're not called to do as the locals do. We're called to do as *Christ* would do. *His* is the culture we're trying to emulate, and his culture most definitely doesn't encourage verbal assault.

WRITING

In the blank space you'll find in the bulletin [or on the index card you received when you entered], write one thing you'd change about our culture if you could.

What is it about our culture that bothers you? Take 60 seconds now to jot it down.

SOURCE: The Associated Press, "Italy Court Rules Insulting Language Part of Life"

Get the Last Word— Guaranteed

TOPIC: Death
SCRIPTURE: Psalm 23:4

POWERPOINT SHOW: Death

If you're someone who likes to have the last word, Robert Barrows has a deal for you.

He's filed a patent application for a hollow tombstone that features a flat touch screen. Activate the screen, and you'll see a video of the dearly departed delivering his or her final words.

Of course, this only works if the person beneath the tombstone has adequate warning that a final message is called for. People who die unexpectedly or who have a change of heart about their final words after leaving a tape with next of kin or a lawyer will be stuck—in *multiple* ways.

WRITING

The fact is we never know which words will be our last words. Statistics indicate that we're all going to die—we just don't know when. And most of us aren't fond of thinking about it.

But let's assume that right now is our last chance to leave words behind, this time in writing. If you had just 60 seconds to jot a note to someone, to whom would you write and what would you say?

Let's find out.

Using the blank space in the bulletin [or on the index card you received when you entered], write your note. You won't have to show it to anyone.

You've got 60 seconds.

Go.

SOURCE: Reuters, "Talking Tombstones to Bear Message From Grave"

Playboy Sent Packing

TOPIC: Discipleship
SCRIPTURE: James 2:14-17

Thanks—but no thanks.

That's what Wesley Britt, a 6'8", 312-pound, all-conference lineman from Alabama, told Playboy magazine when Playboy placed Britt on its preseason All-America football team.

Making the team is quite an honor from a football perspective. Only 22 players are selected, and each enjoys a week in California as well as mention in the magazine.

POWERPOINT SHOW: Discipleship

But Britt, a Christian who often speaks to youth groups and who's committed to living a faithful life, simply didn't feel comfortable accepting the award.

Britt didn't feel it would set a good example—or reflect his beliefs.

 **DISCUSSION**

Britt's decision to turn down Playboy was a decision based on his desire to follow Jesus, not on career development. Turn to a neighbor, and take the next minute to share what you think of Britt's decision.

When a minute has passed, continue.

Now share a discipleship decision *you've* made—a time you chose to be faithful in following Jesus.

SOURCE: The Associated Press, "Alabama's Britt Refuses Playboy Honor"

Girl Grounded, Floorboard Involved

TOPIC: Discipline
SCRIPTURE: Ephesians 6:4

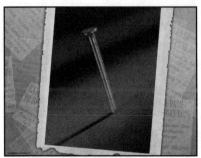

There's discipline…and then there's *discipline*.

Mao Savoeun, a 36-year-old woman living in central Cambodia, wasn't happy with her 13-year-old daughter. Without her mother's consent, the teenager had gone to a Water Festival party at a local pagoda.

So Savoeun grounded her daughter, and I do mean *grounded*.

After the teenager finally came home and fell asleep, Savoeun hammered a two-inch nail through her daughter's right foot, literally nailing the girl to the floorboards.

Savoeun faces investigation and possible criminal charges.

 **DISCUSSION**

Ouch! This makes losing television privileges for the week seem pretty gentle, doesn't it?

Turn to a neighbor, and share your answer to this question:

- **When you were a child, what was the most effective discipline technique used on you?**

SOURCE: Reuters, "Partying Daughter Grounded, Foot Nailed to Floor"

Buns Busted—
Easter Tradition Crumbling

TOPIC: Easter
SCRIPTURE: Matthew 28:7-9

In Great Britain the tradition of serving and eating hot cross buns on Easter dates to 1361. That's when Father Thomas Rockcliffe served the pastry to poor people.

It's important to note that the pastry existed before Father Rockcliffe got involved. The cross on top of the bun represented the four quarters of a moon cycle, and the pastry actually held pagan significance.

POWERPOINT SHOW: Easter

But when Queen Elizabeth I passed a law that hot cross buns could be served only at Christian religious festivals, that sealed the deal: The pastry was officially a Christian symbol.

And that's the problem.

In an effort to avoid offending non-Christian students, school councils across Great Britain have removed hot cross buns from their springtime menus.

Here's the irony: Among hot cross bun supporters is the Muslim Council of Britain, which doesn't view the annual appearance of a pastry as a hate crime.

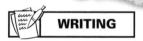

WRITING

Most families have Easter traditions of some sort. Easter eggs, sunrise services, ham dinners. Easter has become an anticipated holiday.

But are our celebrations *Christian* celebrations? Do they focus our attention on Jesus and his empty tomb?

In the blank space provided in your bulletin [or on the card you received when you entered], write a word or two describing an Easter tradition you enjoy—or you've enjoyed in the past. Then take a moment to consider how you could turn that tradition into an intentionally Christian celebration.

SOURCE: Telegraph Group Limited, "Hot Cross Banned: Councils Decree Buns Could Be 'Offensive' to Non-Christians" by Chris Hastings and Elizabeth Day

Smile! You're in Singapore!

TOPIC: Encouragement
SCRIPTURE: 1 Thessalonians 5:11

POWERPOINT SHOW: Encouragement

Want to combat road rage?

Consider encouraging polite drivers by rewarding them with prizes.

That's the philosophy of the government in Singapore, a tiny nation that's launched a Road Courtesy Campaign to make drivers nicer.

Instead of just ticketing inconsiderate motorists, officials have added encouragement to the mix. Drivers who are observed waving to each other, allowing other drivers to merge into heavy traffic, and signaling lane changes early may receive prizes and souvenirs that commemorate their kindness.

Singapore is the same place, by the way, that launched campaigns to encourage citizens to learn proper English and be more romantic.

 **ACTIVITY**

The Singapore government knows something important about encouragement: It takes two for it to happen.

It's tough to be encouraged when you're alone. God has designed us to receive encouragement—and to give it.

Let's do that now. Turn to someone near you, and share an encouraging word. If you know the person, be specific in your encouragement. If you don't know the person, remember that a warm, welcoming smile is an encouragement, too.

Let's take 30 seconds to encourage others.

Go.

SOURCE: The Associated Press, "Singapore Encourages Road Manners"

Spike-Heel Shoes Not Welcome

TOPIC: Evangelism
SCRIPTURE: Matthew 28:18-20

Michael Gill is a British entrepreneur who has a solution for the challenge of getting people to come to church—a significant issue in Great Britain.

If people won't come to the church, Gill intends to take the church to them…literally.

For just $35,000, Gill can provide an inflatable church building that's 47 feet high and contains an inflatable altar and arches.

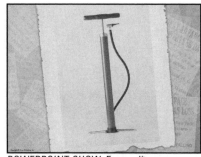

POWERPOINT SHOW: Evangelism

There are even stained-glass windows. Well, they're not actually stained and not really windows. In fact, they're plastic.

Gill suggests the portability of the invention will allow pastors with pickup trucks—and presumably air pumps—to quickly convert any lawn into a church building.

When Jesus encouraged his followers to go to the ends of the earth, one has to wonder if this is what he had in mind.

 **DISCUSSION**

Evangelism is sharing good news—not necessarily erecting a church building on the village green.

If a Christian wanted to encourage neighbors to form a closer friendship with God, what might that Christian do besides spending $35,000 on an inflatable building? Discuss this question with someone seated near you:

- **What might the British church do to encourage people to come to church?**

After a minute or two, continue.

Now talk with the same person about this:

- **In what ways are *we* doing those things—or *not* doing those things—in our own neighborhoods?**

SOURCE: Reuters, "World's 1st Inflatable Church Opens to the Public"

Sun, Sand, and Cigarette Butts

TOPIC: Expectations
SCRIPTURE: James 4:13-15

POWERPOINT SHOW: Expectations

It's July in New Jersey, and every Friday it seems traffic is all headed in one direction: toward the beach.

With 127 miles of coastline, New Jersey offers plenty of oceanfront opportunities for sun, sand, and... cigarette butts.

That's right: cigarette butts. Some 29 *thousand* of them mixed into the beach sand.

In an effort to provide the clean beaches guests and tourists expect, Clean Ocean Action did two beach sweeps in 2003. They collected some interesting debris.

In addition to the 29,907 cigarette butts, 6,199 pieces of lumber, 4,345 pieces of glass, 2,864 bottle caps, and 17,080 straws and stirrers were removed from the beach. There were plenty of other objects, but none I intend to mention.

The result was more of the beach experience people expect: clean sand to go with the warm sun and sparkling water. Everything a beach enthusiast could desire...except the chance to have the beach to himself.

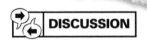 **DISCUSSION**

Turn to someone seated near you, and tell that person a story about a time your expectations weren't met in a restaurant, a store, or an airport.

You'll each have a minute to speak—so if the waiter at the restaurant you visited last week spilled coffee on you, overcharged you, and automatically tacked a 25-percent tip on the bill, you'll probably have to leave out the part of the story where he also served you burnt toast.

Find a partner and share your story.

Ready?

Go.

SOURCE: The Associated Press, "Partial List of Items Found in 2003 Sweeps"

Here's Almost Lookin' at You, Kid

TOPIC: Faith
SCRIPTURE: Hebrews 11:1-3

It's a common story: Boy meets girl while on vacation; boy loses girl when she goes home to Sweden and he goes home to Italy; boy—who's 15—hitchhikes 1,250 miles to see his 17-year-old Swedish dream girl.

Think of it as having faith—faith that the romance was destined to survive; faith that his true love was pining for him just as he was pining for her; faith that no mountain ranges, international boarders, or dangers of the road would stand between them.

Or maybe you should just consider it foolhardy.

The boy was just 110 miles from his Swedish dream girl's house when police picked him up. A quick flurry of phone calls followed, and the girl's father picked up the young man and deposited him at an airport for a sad flight home.

Why?

Because in spite of the young man's faith in the durability of their romance, the girl had already decided enough was enough. She didn't want to see him again.

POWERPOINT SHOW:
Faith 1

SOURCE: Daily Times, "Boy Hitches 1,250 Miles to Rekindle Holiday Romance"

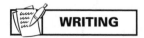 **WRITING**

Is faith really enough to move mountains? Or to at least soften a Swedish girl's heart?

Sometimes we confuse an intense desire to get what *we* want with an intense desire to do what *God* wants. They're not the same. And if mountains are going to be moved, it won't be because those mountains are between us and our goals. They'll be moved because *God* wants the mountains moved and we're cooperating with his mountain-relocation program.

On the space provided in your bulletin [or on the card you received when you entered], briefly write one mountain in your life you'd like God to move.

When you've finished, pray this: "God, let me see clearly if this is a mountain *you* want moved. Help me cooperate with your purposes."

Rock of Ages?

TOPIC: Faith
SCRIPTURE: Matthew 8:25-27

When Steven Wolfe found the rock in an 8-ton load of limestone, he knew he was holding something special. Rather than just another stone, Wolfe saw in the stone the face of Jesus, looking back at him.

POWERPOINT SHOW: Faith 2

Wolfe claims that rubbing the stone has brought both luck and healing in his life. He cites the stone as instrumental in helping his brother and mother conquer cancer, and Wolfe says after his sister and mother touched the stone, they won $600 at Bingo. The rock has been instrumental in strengthening his faith and has brought him good things.

And what do you do when you want to share a gift like this with the world?

You auction it off on eBay.

The rock brought $2,550 at auction.

 **DISCUSSION**

There's a diversity of understanding when it comes to the role faith plays in prompting outcomes. If you have enough faith, can you overcome cancer? raise someone from the dead? quit smoking?

And what happens if you put your faith in the wrong thing? What happens then?

In a moment I'll ask you to turn to someone sitting near you and discuss your answer to this question:

• **What role does faith play in your daily life?**

You'll have two minutes to talk, and I'll let you know when that time is up.

SOURCE: Vindy.com, "Bidding War for Jesus Rock Ends at $2,550"

Some Best Friend

TOPIC: Faithfulness
SCRIPTURE: Proverbs 3:3-4

POWERPOINT SHOW: Faithfulness

The dog: man's best friend and faithful companion.

Yeah, right.

Try explaining that "faithful companion" stuff to goose hunter Michael Boyle.

Boyle and a friend were in a boat on the Columbia River when Boyle shot a goose. As Boyle leaned out of the boat to snag his prize, a dog owned by Boyle's friend stepped on the trigger of a 12-gauge shotgun.

The resulting blast caught Boyle in the leg and sent him to the hospital.

There's no information on the condition of the dog…or Boyle's hunting buddy.

DISCUSSION

I feel blessed to have several faithful friends—and none of them has shot me in the leg.

In a moment I'll ask that you find a partner and share a brief story about a friend of yours—a friend who's been faithful. Answer this question:

- **Who is that person, and how has that friend demonstrated faithfulness to your friendship?**

Find your partner now. Ready to share? You'll have about one minute each. Go.

SOURCE: The Associated Press, "Dog Wounds Goose Hunter With Shotgun"

It's About Time

TOPIC: Forgiveness
SCRIPTURE: Colossians 3:13

Ever felt that you needed to forgive someone? If so, raise your hand.

Ever felt that someone needed to forgive *you*? Raise your hand if that's happened, too.

Forgiveness—authentic forgiveness—can take time.

If you happen to be the city of Istanbul, it can take *800 years*.

POWERPOINT SHOW: Forgiveness

You see, the city of Istanbul was attacked and looted by Crusaders in 1204. In 2001, during a visit to Greece, Pope John Paul II publicly apologized for the Roman Catholic Church's support of the Crusaders' campaign.

And three years later, on the 800th anniversary of Istanbul's fall, Orthodox Christian Patriarch Bartholomew I formally accepted the Pope's apology.

Apology and acceptance are the first steps toward forgiveness…which I hope won't require *another* 800 years.

 **WRITING**

In a moment I'm going to ask you to write something in the blank spot you'll find in the bulletin [or on the card you received when you entered]. Nobody will see what you write.

Please take a moment to write the name of someone whose forgiveness you need. Someone you offended or hurt or ignored. That person may be living or dead; the incident may be recent or have happened long ago.

What's the name?

SOURCE: The Associated Press, "Patriarch Formally Accepts Catholic for Sacking of Constantinople 800 Years Ago"

Kind Words…at a Cost

TOPIC: Friendship
SCRIPTURE: Romans 12:10

POWERPOINT SHOW: Friendship

It's the perfect parting gift for the person who has everything…except friends.

If you're the winner of the Grand Island, Nebraska, Rotary Radio Auction, United Methodist pastor Jim Keyser will come to your funeral and do your eulogy. Bid high, and he'll even say *nice* things about you.

Keyser offered the eulogy when he realized that pastors have few services they can donate for a fundraiser. Apparently few people want an extra sermon or a personal offering plate passed.

But *everyone* wants a kind word spoken at his or her funeral, and some people are willing to pay to guarantee those kind words get spoken.

 **WRITING**

Well, you missed the chance to bid for Keyser's services. That means you'll have to settle for having your actual friends speak about you at your funeral.

Here's a question for you: What do you most want your friends to be able to say? Take a moment to jot down a line or two in the blank space in your bulletin [or on the card you received when you entered]. Nobody will read what you write.

SOURCE: The Associated Press, "Auction Bid Winner to Get Compliments at Funeral"

Cleaning-Supply Employees Clean Up

TOPIC: Generosity
SCRIPTURE: Psalm 112:4-6

In 1950 Charlie Butcher took over the reins of a Massachusetts-based floor-care and cleaning-supplies company his grandfather founded in 1880.

During his long career, Butcher often commented that what made the company successful was its employees. He owed both his corporate and personal success to them.

POWERPOINT SHOW: Generosity

And when Butcher recently sold the company, he put his money where his mouth was.

Butcher divided $18 million among 325 employees.

That's right—$18 *million*.

It may have been September when Butcher's generous checks were handed out, but to Butcher's staff it had to feel like Christmas.

 **ACTIVITY**

Maybe you don't have an extra $18 million to give away today, but you've got something *almost* as good: a welcoming smile and a handshake.

Let's take a moment to give away some of those million-dollar greetings right now. Take a minute to shake three or four hands.

SOURCE: The Associated Press, "Company Shares the Wealth"

So *This* Is the Way the Cookie Crumbles

TOPIC: Giving
SCRIPTURE: Matthew 6:1-4

To Taylor Ostergaard and Lindsey Jo Zellitti, two Colorado teenagers, it seemed the neighborly thing to do.

They teamed up to bake cookies and then delivered the goodies to their neighbors in the rural Durango area. It was their approach that created some difficulties.

The plan was for Ostergaard and Zellitti to wait until after dark, deposit a tray of cookies on a doorstep, then knock on the door, and disappear into the night. When neighbors answered the door, they would be pleasantly surprised.

Unfortunately for the well-intentioned and giving teenagers, when they knocked on the door of Wanita Renea Young, the woman was surprised—but not pleasantly.

Young saw shadowy figures moving outside her house and then heard knocking on the door. When she called out, asking who was outside, the shadows disappeared into the night.

Badly frightened, Young left her house and spent the night with her sister. In the morning, still shaking, Young went to a local hospital.

A Colorado judge has ordered the teenagers to pay nearly $900 to cover Young's medical bills.

Quite a surprise for everyone involved, wasn't it? The good news for the cookie makers is that they've had offers to cover the costs, and they've ended up on media outlets sharing their story.

POWERPOINT SHOW:
Giving 1

SOURCE: The Associated Press, "Cookies for Neighbor Cost Girls $900"

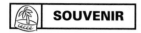 **SOUVENIR**

As a reminder of this story, I've got a surprise for you: a cookie!

Tell your congregation how to collect the cookies—whether the cookies will be served, distributed as the congregation leaves, or picked up at a specific location after the service.

Teacher Gives a Gift That Keeps On Giving

TOPIC: Giving
SCRIPTURE: Galatians 5:13-14

POWERPOINT SHOW: Giving 2

What's the best gift a teacher ever gave you?

Most of us might be able to point to a card, a kind word, or a week's grace for an overdue assignment.

Amy McCloud got a kidney.

When she was 15, McCloud was diagnosed with diabetes, and 20 years later she required 12 hours a week of dialysis as she awaited a kidney transplant. McCloud's relatives weren't medically eligible to provide a kidney.

Then Ron Mercier, who was once McCloud's class adviser and softball coach, heard about McCloud's situation. Mercier, who is 68 years old and retired, shared McCloud's blood type.

And soon McCloud was sharing one of her former teacher's kidneys.

The transplant was performed at the University of Michigan Medical Center.

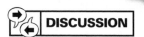 **DISCUSSION**

It takes a special teacher to give a kidney to a student. And while you probably didn't get a kidney from a teacher, perhaps a favorite teacher gave you something else—a vision for your future, a skill you're using today, a friendship that helped you feel good about school.

Turn to someone sitting near you and answer these questions:

• **What's a gift you received from a teacher?**

• **What was special about that gift—and that teacher?**

SOURCE: The Associated Press, "Ex-Mich. Teacher Gives Kidney to Student"

But He Was Making Such Good Time

TOPIC: Goals
SCRIPTURE: Philippians 3:13-14

To Brad Hauter, the roar of an 18-horsepower riding mower is sweet music.

It had better be, because he's driving his mower cross-country. Astride a specially modified mower that boasts top speeds of 25 mph, he's hoping to make the trip from the shadow of the Golden Gate Bridge to within eyeshot of the Statue of Liberty in 79 days.

POWERPOINT SHOW: Goals

Wait…make that *80* days.

The extra time may be required because during the grand send-off on Hauter's first day, his team sent him in the wrong direction. Although he was making good time, in no way was Hauter's course going to get him to New York.

Rather, Hauter was headed for Hawaii.

Course adjustments have been made, and he's on his way.

WRITING

Brad Hauter discovered what most of us have discovered: It doesn't matter if you're making great time if you're headed the wrong direction.

On the space provided for you in the bulletin [or on the card you received when you entered], write one goal you've set for yourself. Maybe it's losing that last 10 pounds or getting that big account at work. Whatever it is, jot yourself a note.

As we explore the idea of goals today, keep in mind the goal you wrote.

SOURCE: San Francisco Chronicle, "Wrong-Way Start to Mowathon; Lawnmower Sets off on Cross-Country Ride" by Steve Rubenstein

I Had It Here Somewhere...

TOPIC: Goodness
SCRIPTURE: Galatians 5:22-23

If you've ever attended the Olympic games, you know the value of pins.

People buy them as collectibles, wear them to show national pride, and take them home as souvenirs. The rarest and most prized pins can soar in value overnight if a particular team or athlete does well in the games.

But the *ultimate* souvenir, the one everyone wants and nobody gets, is an actual Olympic medal. Get your hands on one of *those,* and you can sell it for a fortune.

So imagine the reaction of a taxi driver in Athens who, while cleaning out the back seat of his cab during the 2004 Olympic games, found a silver medal left there by Dutch rower Simon Diederik. Quite a tip.

Except Diederik didn't leave the medal on purpose. That's why an announcement was made to all 5,000 cabbies driving the night the medal was left behind, asking that it be returned.

Diederik didn't know which cab he'd been in or whether a driver or a later passenger found the medal. The cabbie could easily have gotten away with keeping—or selling—the medal.

But he didn't. Instead, the medal was promptly returned to the Olympic Committee and was returned to a grateful and more careful Diederik.

POWERPOINT SHOW:
Goodness

SOURCE: The Associated Press, "Taxi Driver Returns Silver Medal Left in His Cab"

 **ACTIVITY**

To do something good for someone else—something you don't have to do—is a great gift to give. A gift of goodness.

And if the motives are right, it can be an indication of a heart that's being transformed by the power of God.

Let's do something good for someone else right now. In a moment I'll ask you to spend 60 seconds doing something good for someone you know.

That person may be here this morning, and you can share a hug or encouraging word with him or her. Or that person may be far away, in which case you can use the 60 seconds to write that person a note. It's up to you.

Ready?

Go.

Loose Lips Sink Careers

TOPIC: Gossip

SCRIPTURE: Proverbs 16:28

POWERPOINT SHOW: Gossip

Municipal employees in Cascavel, Brazil, should find something to do besides swap gossip at the water coolers.

In fact, they *have* to—or they'll lose their jobs.

The city council has signed into law a statute that makes gossiping by city employees punishable by reprimand, by mandatory sensitivity training, or in some cases by suspension or dismissal.

The city councilman who drafted the legislation hopes it will promote a professional environment and encourage moral integrity.

No word yet on whether it will help city employees actually get more work done.

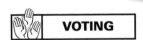 **VOTING**

What is it about gossip that snags our attention so thoroughly? It's next to impossible to resist listening when someone says, "Have you heard about...?"

Or maybe you're one of the strong ones who's never given in to gossip—either sharing it or listening to it.

If you've never been involved in gossip, raise your hand.

Well, I see I'm in the company of honest people—because with few exceptions, we've all fallen prey to gossip.

SOURCE: Reuters, "City Makes Gossip Punishable Offense"

Standing Ovation Brings House Down

TOPIC: Grace
SCRIPTURE: John 1:17

When we think about grace—God's favor given to us even though we don't deserve it—we tend to think of things God does for us.

But God often shows us his grace in what *doesn't* happen.

Just ask Jennifer Flanagan.

Representative Flanagan is a Massachusetts lawmaker. During the governor's State of the State address, she joined her colleagues in a standing ovation.

Good thing, too.

While Flanagan stood applauding, the glass cover of a ceiling light fixture above her fell, smashing into her chair. Had Flanagan been seated, she might well have been killed.

Today we're all facing challenges. Yet, as we sit here, no ceiling lights are crashing onto our heads. No meteorites are ripping through the roof. No volcanoes are exploding beneath our feet.

There's grace around us. Perhaps we don't see it in the special favors God is granting us to make our lives easier or pain-free. But we can certainly see it in what's *not* happening in our lives.

POWERPOINT SHOW:
Grace

SOURCE: The New York Times Company, "Light Fixture Falls From House Ceiling, Nearly Hitting Lawmaker"

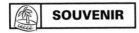 **SOUVENIR**

As people arrive, distribute a small, inexpensive metal bolt to each. You'll ask people to tuck these pieces of hardware into their pockets, so don't substitute screws or nails; your congregation won't thank you later!

As you came into the room today, you received one of these—a bolt that's used to keep things together. When you see a bolt, you know that it's there for a good reason and removing it may well create problems!

Tuck your bolt into a pocket. Let it be a reminder of all the things in your life that *aren't* falling apart. God's grace is all around us—though we often don't recognize it.

Ready...Aim...Riot

TOPIC: Greed
SCRIPTURE: Luke 12:15

Picture this: A real estate investor decides to give away $10,000 at a St. Petersburg, Florida, mall.

He's going to stand on a balcony overlooking the mall courtyard while a crowd of approximately 500 anxious people waits below.

The investor, Kevin Shelton, will then aim a "cash cannon" over the elbowing crowd and blast 5,000 two-dollar bills overhead, literally blanketing the crowd in a blizzard of bills.

What could possibly go wrong?

Greed could enter the picture, that's what.

When the cash-blast exploded in midair, the crowd went crazy. People dove, snatched, grabbed, and trampled each other as they waved upside-down umbrellas trying to capture cash floating down like confetti. Six people were hospitalized, and another half-dozen treated on the scene for cuts and bruises.

The mall is evaluating the event, determining if something should have been done differently.

POWERPOINT SHOW:
Greed 1

SOURCE: The Associated Press, "12 Injured in Fight for $10K Launched Into Mall Crowd"

 **SOUVENIR**

As people enter the room, distribute a nickel to each one.

Picture yourself in that St. Petersburg mall.

Now imagine that Shelton is tossing a solitary nickel to the crowd below. How hard would the crowd scrape and fight to get the nickel?

Not much. Five cents doesn't inspire much greed.

But $10,000? *That* obviously did the trick. It's not money that kicks our greed into overdrive; it's the idea that we might be able to get and control a great *deal* of money. Greed isn't just about money; it's about gaining more of what money can buy.

And you won't get much with that nickel you just received.

Put the nickel you received today in a pocket where you don't usually carry change. When you next see it, let it remind you that money is just money. Having a nickel doesn't have to inspire greed.

Having $10 doesn't have to inspire greed.

And neither does having $10,000.

Taxi Greed Gains Ground

TOPIC: Greed
SCRIPTURE: 1 Timothy 6:9-10

Prague's mayor, Pavel Bem, had heard the rumors that the city's taxi drivers sometimes overcharged tourists. At the urging of an area journalist, the mayor decided to check out the charges himself.

POWERPOINT SHOW: Greed 2

Mayor Bem disguised himself as a tourist and hailed a cab at Prague's Old Town Square for a 1.8-mile trip to Prague Castle. Both locations are popular tourist destinations.

Bem expected to pay top dollar—the official rate capped by law—and perhaps even a bit more. Maybe even a *lot* more, up to 100 percent more than could be legally charged.

But in his wildest dreams, the mayor didn't expect to be charged 500 percent of the official rate. The mayor's tab for the less than 2-mile trip: $34.17.

More than likely, that didn't include a tip.

 **INTERVIEW**

Well before the service, contact several people, and ask to interview them. Confirm that they'll be in attendance, and share the questions you'll ask.

All of us have felt greedy a time or two…or perhaps even more often. And usually greed doesn't bring out the best in us or in our relationships with God.

I've asked our panel here to answer a couple of questions about greed. Please note that I didn't select them to be interviewed because I think they're especially greedy—just the opposite, in fact. But if they're human, they've confronted greed at least once.

- **In what situation did you see greed creep into your life?**

- **What impact did greed have on you?**

SOURCE: Reuters, "Notorious Taxis Take Mayor for a Ride"

Robber Requests Do-Over

TOPIC: Guilt
SCRIPTURE: John 16:7-8

When a gunman wearing a ski mask entered the Okagaki branch of Japan's Onga Shinkin Bank, he made an unauthorized withdrawal: more than 1.5 million yen in 10,000-yen notes.

The gunman fled and escaped in a black car.

But less than a week later, the bank received a parcel delivery that contained nearly all the money, along with an apology.

It seemed the robber had committed the crime on an impulse and regretted both the crime and the extra work it had created for bank employees. In

his note, the robber admitted that returning the money probably wouldn't erase his crime, but perhaps it would make him feel better about having committed it.

POWERPOINT SHOW:
Guilt

SOURCE: The Mainichi Newspapers Co., "Remorseful Robber Posts Stolen Money Back to Bank"

 **WRITING**

A guilty robber…and one who's willing to do something to relieve his guilt.

If we're honest, we probably have to admit we know how he feels. We've all done things we're happy nobody else knows about.

And those things often cause us to experience guilt.

Here's the thing: We don't *have* to live with guilt. We can be forgiven by God, and—perhaps—by the people we've wronged. There are consequences to our actions, certainly, and I'm guessing if the robber is caught, the Japanese penal system will have one more inmate.

But what would it be worth to feel forgiveness? For our consciences to let us breathe freely again?

On the blank space in your bulletin [or on the card you received when you arrived], jot down these words: "I can be forgiven." Then look at them, written in your own hand. Those words are true—but only if you're willing to confess what you've done to God.

Are you willing? What's it worth to you?

Iron-Rich Diet Proves Problematic

TOPIC: Habits
SCRIPTURE: Galatians 6:7

POWERPOINT SHOW: Habits

Scrubbing under our fingernails, wiping our shoes on a mat before we go into the house, brushing after each meal. Those are the sorts of everyday habits that can make our lives easier because they help us do positive things automatically.

But other habits don't always benefit us.

Consider an Ethiopian man named Gezahenge Debebe. Forty-year-old Debebe has apparently been swallowing metal for the past 20 years. A *lot* of metal.

Doctors removed 222 nails, keys, and coins that he swallowed. That's some 26 ounces of items, most of them rusted.

Debebe is recovering in the hospital.

Here's hoping doctors are keeping all those metal surgical instruments out of sight.

 **DISCUSSION**

We've all got habits. Some are endearing and charming. Others aren't.

It's time to 'fess up. Turn to someone sitting near you, and tell that person one habit of yours that might—just *might*—aggravate other people just a teensy bit. Not that it's a *bad* habit, of course; probably those people who get annoyed are too easily aggravated.

Take a moment now. I can wait. I'd confess an aggravating habit of my own, but, well, I just don't have any.

SOURCE: Reuters, "Doctors Remove 222 Nails From Man's Belly"

Runner Takes Caffeine to Go

TOPIC: Health
SCRIPTURE: 1 Corinthians 6:19-20

Here's a blood test most of us wouldn't want to take.

In the Dominican Republic, a runner from Surinam was stripped of her gold medal at the Pan American Games. The reason: excessive caffeine in her system.

POWERPOINT SHOW: Health

Letitia Vriesde ran for her country in the 2000 Olympics and has been a silver and bronze medalist in other world-championship events. So it was no great surprise that she won the 800-meter event.

What *was* a surprise was the amount of caffeine in her system.

You might expect an athlete to enjoy a diet cola or a cappuccino now and then. And perhaps the caffeine taken in through a drink might spike a bit of improvement in a runner's performance.

But the Pan American Sports Organization president estimated that the amount of caffeine in the runner's blood would have required Vriesde to drink five *gallons* of coffee.

That's an amount of caffeine that not even the most dedicated Starbucks fan can hope to imbibe. In addition to violating a Pan American Games standard, that amount of caffeine can pose a serious health risk.

 **SOUVENIR**

Before your congregation arrives, place a piece of individually wrapped chocolate on each chair. People will have to interact with the chocolate before they take their seats.

On your seat you found a piece of chocolate. It's a gift…and it's loaded with caffeine. If you didn't find a piece of chocolate, look at your neighbor. If he or she looks guilty…

Here's my point: A little chocolate, a little caffeine, a little saturated fat—they're all usually acceptable in a healthy lifestyle. But too much of nearly anything creates problems—and compromises health.

SOURCE: The Associated Press, "Caffeine Jolts Runner From Victory"

No Good Deed Goes Unpunished

TOPIC: Helping Others
SCRIPTURE: Galatians 6:2

POWERPOINT SHOW: Helping Others

In Owasso, Oklahoma, Doug Jones has discovered the cost of being a good Samaritan after a snowstorm.

It's $117, and it comes in the form of a traffic ticket.

Here's what happened...

Jones has a Jeep, and when a snowstorm sent motorists along U.S. 169 into ditches, Jones showed up to help out. He pulled a friend's car out of the rough and then just kept going. Jones found another stranded motorist, hooked the car to his Jeep, and got that grateful driver back on the road.

Jones had the Jeep, and he had the time, and when an Oklahoma Highway Patrol car pulled in behind him, lights flashing, he figured he even had some help.

Not quite.

It turns out that enthusiastic good Samaritans can sometimes cause accidents on the highway. So as good as their intentions are, they're discouraged from creating hazards.

Discouraged to the tune of $117.

Not to fear, though. Oklahomans sympathetic to Jones' situation have protested on his behalf and have even offered to pay the fine for him.

 **ACTIVITY**

Helping others requires a couple of things: someone to help and a willingness to get involved.

Let's take a practical look at a way you and I might be able to help others. I've asked our children's pastor [or another staff member representing a ministry that needs volunteers] to tell us about ways our children's ministry could use some help.

As you listen for the next two minutes, ask yourself: Is this a way I can help others?

SOURCE: The Associated Press, "Good Samaritan Faces $117 Traffic Fine"

Hopeful Treasure Hunters Swarm School Ground

TOPIC: Hope
SCRIPTURE: Romans 12:12

OK, so it's a long shot…but one a surprising number of people are taking.

Armed with shovels and high hopes, people are showing up at a demolition site in Windsor, Ontario, digging for buried treasure.

Fifty years ago, Marty Gervais and two friends filled a tin with childhood treasures and buried the tin near their school. They tossed in a Davy Crockett

POWERPOINT SHOW: Hope

coonskin cap, and among the other items was a baseball card…a 1952 Topps Mickey Mantle rookie card.

No one cares about the cap, but if the Mickey Mantle card is still in top condition, it's worth hundreds of thousands of dollars.

Gervais is a newspaper columnist, and now that the school is being demolished, he's shared his story. And apparently he has readers, because so many treasure hunters are showing up that the demolition company has had to hire security guards.

WRITING

Most of us have hope—hope for a financial windfall, for our children's college prospects, or for good health.

And that hope gives us a vision for the future.

My question for you: What do you hope for?

On the space provided in your bulletin [or on the card you received when you arrived], take a moment to write something that gives you hope in your life.

SOURCE: CBC, "Baseball Card Draws Fortune Hunters to Ontario School"

Losing Streak a Record

TOPIC: Humility
SCRIPTURE: Micah 6:8

POWERPOINT SHOW: Humility

In Indiana, basketball is a sort of unofficial religion.

And in *this* religion, winning is everything.

So you can imagine how it felt to play on the girls' basketball team at the Daleville High School in Daleville, Indiana. It's a single-A school with less than 200 students, one of Indiana's smallest high schools.

The mighty fighting Broncos had set a school record—for losing. And not just a school record; it was a conference and division record, too. In fact, it was an Indiana *state* record: 113 straight losses.

It took six *years* for the girls' team to get beat that many times.

But take heart: The sun is shining bright in Daleville, Indiana, these days. The girls' team trounced Fort Wayne Keystone with a score of 61-27.

Fans aren't making reservations for the playoffs just yet, though. With the win the girls' team now has a season with 1 win…and 17 losses.

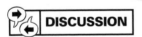 **DISCUSSION**

Ouch. It must have been humbling to walk onto the court game after game and get beaten so often. You've got to wonder what the coach found to say at halftime.

It's humbling to be beaten, and most of us *hate* being humbled.

In a moment, I'm going to ask you to turn to someone seated near you and to answer this question:

• **When were you humbled?**

Introduce yourself, and answer that question. You've got two minutes.
Go.

SOURCE: The Associated Press, "Team Ends 113-Game Losing Streak"

Broker Discovers
He Has a Second Job

TOPIC: Identity in Christ
SCRIPTURE: 2 Corinthians 5:17

When children who've been adopted search for their birth parents, they're never certain what they'll find.

Marty Johnson, a mortgage broker in Minnesota, found more than he bargained for. A *lot* more.

A few years ago, Johnson's birth mother contacted him and filled Johnson in on a few details concerning his background. Among those details was

POWERPOINT SHOW: Identity in Christ

this: Johnson's father was Nigerian and had been a master's degree candidate at Northern Iowa University.

That was enough for Johnson to make some connections in Nigeria. He discovered that not only was his father still living, but his father was a chief. Prior to Nigeria's adoption of a centralized government, Johnson's ancestors were sufficiently powerful to declare and go to war with other tribal groups.

As the chief's eldest son, Johnson now finds himself in line to become the next chief, though he's never been to Nigeria a day in his life.

 **ACTIVITY**

When it comes to identity, lots of people tell us who we are.

Our roles as parents, employees, bosses, friends, homeowners or renters, members of clubs and associations—they're all outlined in our wallets and purses.

Pull out your wallet—I promise no offering plate will be coming around—and choose one card or other item that you think describes part of your identity that matters to you. Take 30 seconds.

Now, think about your identity as a child of God. What do you see in your wallet or purse that reminds you that you're God's child?

Is it there? What do you carry that reminds you of your identity in the kingdom of God?

SOURCE: The Associated Press, "Minn. Man Discovers He's a Nigerian Prince"

Wink Proves Costly

TOPIC: Jealousy
SCRIPTURE: Romans 13:12-14

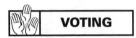 **VOTING**

My name is [insert your name here], and I have a confession to make: I've been jealous a time or two in my life.

Raise your hand if you've experienced jealousy, too. Thank you.

And how many of you were ever inspired to do something positive when you were feeling jealous? Raise your hands.

Hmm...fewer hands this time.

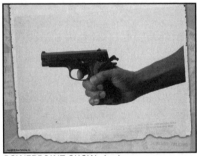

POWERPOINT SHOW: Jealousy

Jealousy isn't one of those emotions that brings out the best in us.

That was certainly true of Andrew Morton, a 16-year-old who shot and killed another 16-year-old boy in Milwaukee. The victim, Justin Simpson, committed a crime that resulted in his on-the-spot execution.

Simpson's crime? He allegedly winked at Morton's girlfriend and blew her a kiss.

That's all it took.

Simpson was shot in the head, shoulder, and chest and died of his wounds.

SOURCE: The Associated Press, "Teen Allegedly Killed Boy for Winking at Girlfriend"

Joyful, Joyful…Wait… We *Abhor* Thee, Ultramar

TOPIC: Joy
SCRIPTURE: Psalm 30:4-5

Suppose you were to win one of three grand prizes in a drawing, and the grand prize was worth $1,500 in gas for your car. Wouldn't that make you happy? *I'd* be happy to win that prize.

Now suppose that *you* won one of the three grand prizes and so did 100,000 of your New Brunswick neighbors. Having that many happy people around would turn New Brunswick into Joyful Central. Lots of smiles and high fives; it'd be a great day in New Brunswick.

And if you've been doing the math, it would also be a *confusing* day. One hundred thousand people can't all win a grand prize if there are only three grand prizes, right?

Well, they can if there's been a printing error.

Ultramar, a Canadian gasoline retailer, distributed 314,000 contest coupons in New Brunswick. A misprint made 100,000 of those coupons winners of the $1,500 grand prize. This came as something of a shock to the company, which was planning to give away $4,500 in gasoline.

Instead, Ultramar owed $150 million in gasoline.

The good news for the company—if not the 100,000 winners—is that because the contest rules said there would be only three grand-prize winners, the company won't have to honor all the winning coupons.

Just three. But I wonder *which* three.

POWERPOINT SHOW:
Joy

SOURCE: CANOE, "Ultramar Voids Erroneous Coupons"

 **WRITING**

For most of us, our happiness depends to a large degree on our circumstances. You may be feeling a bit grumpy, but win a coupon worth $1,500 in gasoline, and your attitude is going to improve *dramatically*.

But joy...joy *doesn't* depend on circumstances. It's defined not by us, but by God.

In the space provided in your bulletin [or on the card you received when you entered], write one thing that brings you joy: authentic, sunny-even-on-a-cloudy-morning joy. You won't have to share what you write with anyone, so be honest.

Where's your joy?

So Much for Honor Among Thieves

TOPIC: Justice
SCRIPTURE: Psalm 9:16

It started when nine Vietnamese criminals used cow fat and paint to make a lump of iron resemble a piece of black bronze—expensive metal used to make fine jewelry and art objects.

The criminals found three business people in Ho Chi Minh City who were willing to buy the fake bronze. And that's what the business people did... using counterfeit money.

POWERPOINT SHOW: Justice

When the fake-bronze makers started spending counterfeit bills from the 900 million Vietnamese dong they'd received (worth about $58,000 US), they were promptly arrested. That led to the arrest of the counterfeiters, and Vietnamese courts are sorting it out from there.

I don't know the penalty for counterfeiting bronze, but counterfeiting bills carries a stiff sentence in Vietnam—anything from three years in prison to execution by firing squad.

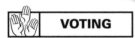 **VOTING**

Who was the victim here?

The bronze counterfeiters who ended up in jail because they were paid in counterfeit bills? Raise your hand if you think they were victims.

How about the businessmen who paid in fake bills but who got fake bronze? Raise your hand if you think they were victims.

How about the Vietnamese government, who had to deal with 900 million dong in counterfeit money? Raise your hand if you think the government was a victim.

It appears we don't have a great deal of agreement on this. I hope the Vietnamese justice system has an easier time sorting out who's to blame!

SOURCE: Reuters, "Man Sells Fake Bronze, Gets Paid in Counterfeit"

Is Kindness Genetic?

TOPIC: Kindness
SCRIPTURE: Ephesians 4:32

POWERPOINT SHOW: Kindness 1

Why is it that some people seem to be naturally kind—and others aren't?

Is kindness a spiritual issue alone, or might there be something else... something connected to genetics?

Psychologist Philippe Ruston of the University of Western Ontario in London, Ontario, has authored a study on altruism, and he believes there's a genetic connection to being kind and giving.

Ruston analyzed data he collected from 174 pairs of identical twins, who share an identical genetic makeup, and 148 pairs of fraternal twins, who share only half their genetic makeup.

Participants completed a 22-question survey that dealt with moral issues. Ruston hypothesized that identical twins would agree twice as often as fraternal twins on moral issues if genetics were influencing their choices—and that's what happened.

Ruston's study isn't the final word on whether kindness is genetic, though. Some critics point out other factors might account for Ruston's findings.

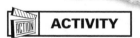 **ACTIVITY**

As for me, I don't really care if genetics makes one person more likely than another to be kind. At heart, *all* of us need help in the kindness department.

Let's stretch those kindness muscles now.

In a moment I'll ask that we all stand and spend 30 seconds being kind to at least one other person. How you do that—with a smile, a handshake, or a quick backrub—I'll leave up to you and the person to whom you're being kind.

But let's give it a try. Ready?

Go.

SOURCE: ABC News Internet Ventures, "Are We Programmed for Kindness?"

A Tree That's Tops

TOPIC: Kindness
SCRIPTURE: Galatians 5:22-23

The tree outside the Dawes County, Nebraska, courthouse had to go.

So in far less time than it took the stately tree to grow, it was removed—leaving only an unsightly stump.

A big, unsightly stump.

A big, unsightly stump that was somehow transformed into a sculpture.

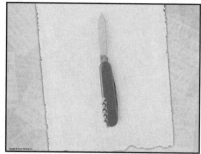

POWERPOINT SHOW: Kindness 2

Courthouse workers were surprised to discover the Blind Lady of Justice carved into the stump. They appreciated the kind gesture and liked the art-work—a lot.

They just didn't know whom to thank since the artwork was unsigned.

The courthouse workers placed a thank-you letter in the local newspaper, the Chadron Record, and they soon received a response.

Christine Osterman, a college student, admitted she was the sculptor. Unobserved—or at least unreported—she'd used a chainsaw to do the carving.

 **WRITING**

Giving a piece of art—even art carved in a stump—is a kind act. It was a kindness that encouraged the county workers in Dawes County.

Kindness is encouraging, isn't it? When people are kind to us, it adds spring to our steps and smiles to our faces.

In the blank spot in your bulletin [or on the card you received when you entered], jot a quick description of a kindness someone did for you. When were you the recipient of God's love, directed to you through another person?

SOURCE: The Associated Press, "Old Tree Becomes Work of Art"

Watch Out for That First Step

TOPIC: Leadership
SCRIPTURE: Luke 14:27

POWERPOINT SHOW: Leadership

We expect a lot from our leaders. At minimum, we expect that they'll provide good direction.

So you can imagine how readers felt when the advice given by Trail magazine, Britain's leading hiking magazine with a circulation of 36,000, recommended a route that takes hikers straight off a cliff.

Scotland's Ben Nevis, Britain's tallest peak at 4,406 feet, has a wicked north face, and several hikers have lost their lives there.

Trail magazine thought it would be helpful to provide directions that would safely lead hikers down the mountain in bad weather. Unfortunately, the first of two critical bearings was deleted during the editing process.

The editor of the magazine, Guy Procter, has apologized for the mistake and pointed out that few if any hikers would attempt that trail without a detailed map in hand.

Good thing, too, or those hikers might find that getting down the mountain will take *far* less time than they'd expected.

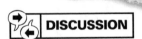

DISCUSSION

Playing Follow the Leader works only if the leader is worth following. Otherwise it might turn into a game of "that first step was a real doozy."

Turn to someone sitting near you, and tell that person about a time *you* got less-than-adequate directions from someone you considered a leader.

Maybe it was something simple, like a hiking book telling you to dive off a cliff. Or maybe it was something more complicated. What you share is up to you, but here's the question:

• **When did a leader let you down?**

SOURCE: The Associated Press, "Technical Difficulties in Scotland!"

No News Is Good News

TOPIC: Legalism
SCRIPTURE: Matthew 23:25-27

When Pennsylvania high school junior Laurie Hanniford received a certified letter, it wasn't good news.

Hanniford, 17, had worked as a part-time swim instructor three years earlier and earned a total of $316. From that amount she'd paid the required $3.16 in local taxes.

Unfortunately, she'd failed to file a local tax return.

POWERPOINT SHOW: Legalism

Three years later, acting on behalf of Hanniford's local municipality, the Capital Tax Collection Bureau had a district justice issue a criminal complaint. Hanniford was fined $352 for failing to submit the paperwork—a fine that was $36 *more* than she'd earned at her job.

Hanniford pled no contest, and her fine was reduced to $77.

 **DISCUSSION**

Obey the letter of the law—that seems to be the attitude of the tax collectors in Laurie Hanniford's life.

And here's what's odd: As unfair as it may seem to Hanniford, she *did* in fact break the law when she didn't turn in paperwork. And the stiff fine she faced will certainly be memorable—she'll never forget again.

In a moment, I'm going to ask you to turn to someone seated near you and to share a story from your own life. When were you unfairly punished by the letter of the law?

Maybe you were grounded for a week because you got home one minute after curfew. Or you parked exactly 2 inches over the line in a parking lot and received a ticket.

- **When were you punished by the letter of the law…and how did that feel?**

Find a partner, and take a minute to share your story.

SOURCE: The Associated Press, "Teen Fined for Not Filing $3 Tax Bill" by Marc Levy

Hibberts Gore, Maine: Population 1

TOPIC: Loneliness
SCRIPTURE: Genesis 2:18

POWERPOINT SHOW: Loneliness 1

There's loneliness, and there's being alone—and they aren't necessarily the same.

Consider Karen Keller, who is the sole resident of Hibberts Gore, Maine.

In the 2000 census, Keller is listed as the only person living in a 640-acre section of northern Maine that remains unincorporated, claimed by no county. In a rush to survey the area, the plot was apparently ignored by surveyors.

Hibberts Gore has no library. No street lights. No electricity or running water. There's nothing there but Keller's cabin and Keller, who was also Hibberts Gore's lone resident during the 1990 census.

At present, Keller expresses no interest in moving to a more populated area.

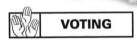

VOTING

For some of us, the notion of being alone 24/7 is a horrible thought. We need to be around people and modern distractions.

For others here, a few weeks of solitary sounds about right.

If you would welcome two weeks in the Maine woods—alone, raise your hand.

If you think you would perish without friends and a phone, raise *your* hand.

And how many of you are surprised to see which answer your spouse gave? Raise *your* hands.

I'll have a sign-up sheet for marital counseling in the back after the service...

SOURCE: Boston Globe Newspaper Company, "Population: 1" by Cindy Rodriguez

Who Said Talk Was Cheap?

TOPIC: Loneliness
SCRIPTURE: Ecclesiastes 4:11

 VOTING

How many of you have ever felt lonely? Raise your hands.

Those of you who didn't raise your hands must have never spent a week at camp when you were in third grade.

Those of you who *have* at times felt lonely probably haven't been as lonely as a 28-year-old German man. Here's his story.

When his cell phone rang, he was intrigued to discover the caller was a woman who called herself Tina.

Tina said she'd found the man's name on the Internet and would like to talk with him. Tina provided a number where she could be reached if the man called right back.

The man did so, and the two spent six hours talking.

POWERPOINT SHOW: Loneliness 2

Six hours.

It must have been quite a conversation.

But no matter what they discussed or how happy he was to have connected with Tina, the man was unhappy to later receive a $7,244 phone bill.

He hadn't been *that* lonely, and police are considering charges of fraud against the woman.

SOURCE: Reuters, "All Night Phone Flirt Costs a Fortune"

Parents Call License Shots

TOPIC: Love
SCRIPTURE: Ephesians 4:14-15

POWERPOINT SHOW: Love

Call it "tough love."

Parents in Georgia may soon find themselves with more power to keep their teenagers from driving poorly. Instead of just taking the car keys, parents will be able to pull their kids' driver's licenses as well.

If a bill introduced in Atlanta passes, parents will be able to send $15 to the Department of Motor Vehicle Services and request that their child's license be suspended from 90 days up to the child's 18th birthday. The duration of the suspension will be up to the parent.

The goal is to see a decrease in traffic accidents and deaths associated with young drivers—and giving parents the power to pull licenses is viewed as one way to accomplish that goal.

Will pulling a license make Mom or Dad popular? Probably not, but it may be the most loving thing to do for a young driver who hasn't discovered the value of driving slowly or obeying stop signs.

 **DISCUSSION**

When you're a parent, love doesn't always mean doing the popular thing. It means doing the *loving* thing, doing what's best for the child you love.

Turn to someone sitting near you and share your answer to this question:

- **When did someone tell you something that was difficult for you to hear—but it was the best thing for you?**

You'll have two minutes to share.

SOURCE: The Associated Press, "New Rules Possible for Teen Drivers"

No *Wonder* You Look Familiar

TOPIC: Loyalty
SCRIPTURE: Proverbs 28:20a

Most businesses depend on the loyalty of customers, and Cawood Buick Pontiac Honda in Port Huron, Michigan, is no exception.

So you can imagine how pleased the car dealership is with John Gathergood, a repeat Buick buyer.

A *very* repeat buyer, actually.

Gathergood, who's 82, recently purchased his 30th new Buick at the same dealership.

POWERPOINT SHOW: Loyalty

He picked out his first Buick in 1939, and Gathergood is still a fan. His latest car is a black Buick that cost $42,000.

 **ACTIVITY**

OK, let's see what sort of loyalty we have here among car buyers.

If you've purchased two or more cars from the same dealer or from the same car lot, stand up, please.

If you've purchased *three* or more, stay standing.

Continue raising the number until you've eliminated everyone. It's highly unlikely you'll reach 30 or more!

SOURCE: The Associated Press, "Man Buys 30th Buick From Same Dealer"

"K Syndrome" Less Fatal Than Assumed

TOPIC: Lying

SCRIPTURE: Ephesians 4:15

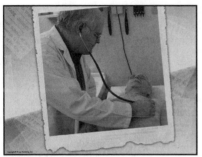

POWERPOINT SHOW: Lying

Lying is wrong. Not only did your mother say so, but God mentioned it prominently in the Ten Commandments.

But is lying *always* wrong? Is there *never* a time you should bend the rule?

Consider the lie told by Vittorio Sacerdoti, an Italian doctor who lied to save the lives of 45 Roman Jews.

As Nazis entered the Jewish ghetto in Italy where he lived, Dr. Sacerdoti—himself a Jew—gathered as many Jews as possible into the small hospital where he worked. He admitted the Jews as patients and indicated on their medical charts that they suffered from "K Syndrome."

Nazis who came to collect the patients found them coughing violently, victims of an apparently deadly and contagious disease.

Afraid of contracting K Syndrome, the Nazis fled—and didn't return.

As you've already guessed, there's no such thing as K Syndrome. Dr. Sacerdoti's invention and coaching saved the lives of his Jewish neighbors…but the good doctor had to lie to do it.

Would it have been better to have told the Nazis the truth?

WRITING

On the space in your bulletin [or on the card you received when you entered], write your answer—your honest answer—to this question:

- **Was Dr. Sacerdoti's lie justified?**

No one will see what you write unless you choose to reveal it, so answer as honestly as you can. And remember your answer as we move more deeply into the message.

SOURCE: BBC News, "Italian Doctor Who Fooled Nazis"

What Women Want... And Guys, Too

TOPIC: Marriage
SCRIPTURE: Colossians 3:18-19

Maybe you think it's no big deal that you've put off picking up those dirty dishes stashed under the sofa. Or that the arguments you and your spouse have over money aren't worth a second thought. Think again.

According to a report presented at the American Sociological Association's annual meeting, happiness in marriage can be torpedoed by money arguments and failing to do a fair share of household tasks.

POWERPOINT SHOW: Marriage

Juliana McGene, a doctoral candidate, analyzed data gathered from 860 couples. She measured dissatisfaction by how often the couples reported fighting, whether they considered their marriages in trouble, and whether they'd considered divorce.

McGene found that when spouses perceive their partners are ducking a fair share of chores or being irresponsible with money, marriage satisfaction suffers.

Make a note: If you're married and you want a more satisfying marriage, pick up those dishes. Balance that checkbook.

And do a load of laundry while you're at it.

 VOTING

If you're here and you're married, it's time to take a vote.

If you think you could do a better job with chores, raise your hand...

If you think your money management could be improved at least a little, raise your hand...

If you think your spouse is pretty much wonderful just as he or she is, raise your hand...

There—*that's* how to have a happy marriage!

SOURCE: Reuters, "Division of Household Chores Affects Marital Bliss"

Sticks and Stones
May Break My Bones…

TOPIC: Mercy
SCRIPTURE: Matthew 5:7

Remember middle school? Or maybe it was called junior high back in your day.

Did anyone ever call you a name? Or hang an embarrassing nickname on you? Raise your hand if name-calling was a part of your preteen experience. And don't worry—I'm not going to ask you to share what those names *were*.

Name-calling has been so common for so long it seems as natural a part of the middle school years as hormones and homework. But for a week in January, in some schools name-calling will be mercifully absent.

No one's sure how many middle schools will get on board for "No Name-Calling Week," but more than 5,100 educators registered in January 2005.

That means that, in at least 5,000 classrooms, insults about children's appearance, behavior, and background will be silenced for five school days.

For any student singled out because he's different, those will be five days of mercy. Five days when the conversation is compassionate, not critical.

For any student singled out because she's not different *enough*, those will be five days of mercy. Five days when words are caring, not cruel.

Here's hoping that No Name-Calling Week stretches out to No Name-Calling Month, or No Name-Calling Year.

We can all use a little more mercy in our lives.

POWERPOINT SHOW:
Mercy

SOURCE: The Associated Press, "Conservatives Criticize National 'No Name-Calling' Week"

WRITING

Nicknames we'd rather no one know—we've all had them. Names we wish would disappear forever. Can you recall one that other kids hung on you?

Good.

Do this: In the space provided in your bulletin [or on the card you received when you entered], please do *not* write that name down. Take a pen or pencil, and look at that blank space where the name you hated so much years ago could appear—and don't write it there.

We're children of God and treat each other that way. Here it's *always* No Name-Calling Week.

Ask and Ye Shall Receive…
Unfortunately

TOPIC: Miracles
SCRIPTURE: Luke 19:37-38

POWERPOINT SHOW: Miracles

Miracle? You decide.

At a First Baptist Church in Hardin County, Ohio, an evangelist was preaching up a storm—at the same time a storm thundered away outside. At one point the preacher asked for a sign from God.

Immediately a bolt of lightning hit the church steeple, blasting out the sound system. The lightning traveled through the church wiring, shocking the evangelist.

After determining the evangelist wasn't injured, the worship service continued but then stopped again when someone realized the building was on fire. The church building was evacuated, and the fire department extinguished the blaze.

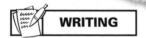

WRITING

God does work in mysterious ways, but setting a building on fire as a sign might be a bit suspect. God could easily have chosen to send a sign that was less destructive if he were inclined to send signs.

A question: *Does* God work in the world today? Is he in the business of providing signs or manipulating outcomes?

On the blank area in your bulletin [or on the card you received when you entered], answer that question.

• **How does God work in the world today?**

Nobody will see your answer unless you choose to show it to someone.

SOURCE: The Associated Press, "Lightning Hits as Preacher Asks for Sign From God"

Missions Tragedy...Again

TOPIC: Missions
SCRIPTURE: Mark 16:15

Mohan Kumar, an actor portraying the martyred missionary Graham Staines, was burned alive while staging a re-enactment of Mr. Staines' death.

Staines and his two sons died in India in 1998 when the jeep in which they were sleeping was set on fire by a mob, allegedly led by a Hindu zealot.

Kumar, playing the role of Staines, had doused himself with gasoline—a

POWERPOINT SHOW: Missions

nod toward realism not explained to his fellow actors. One of the other cast members lit a match near Kumar, who was immediately engulfed in flames in full view of the nearly 1,000 members of the audience.

Kumar was rushed to a hospital in Madras, India, where he died of injuries sustained in the incident.

 VOTING

Graham Staines died in service of the kingdom, a missionary who laid his life down on the mission field.

A tragedy? Certainly...but not entirely unexpected.

Christians die every day for their faith, usually unheralded and unknown...at least on Earth. In heaven, it's another matter.

You—like me—have two decisions to make.

The first is sobering: Would you be willing to die in service of the King? Staines answered yes to that question by being on the mission field and being outspoken about his faith.

The second question is one that I'll invite you to vote on by standing where you are if you're willing to answer yes. The question is this:

• **Are you willing to *live* for your faith?**

If the answer is yes, would you join me in standing?

SOURCE: BBC NEWS, "Actor Dies Recreating Missionary Murder"

And She's Outta Here… Almost

TOPIC: Modesty
SCRIPTURE: 1 Timothy 2:9-10

POWERPOINT SHOW: Modesty

When Amina Khabab, a 32-year-old camera operator employed by 2M television, showed up for work, she was wearing denim jeans and a T-shirt.

No problem, right?

Wrong.

Ms. Khabab was filming a parliamentary session in Morocco where it's customary for women to wear veils in many settings. Settings that include the parliament, apparently, because an angry Islamist member of parliament rose and demanded Ms. Khabab be expelled from the parliamentary chamber.

Her clothing, the angry MP claimed, was an invitation to debauchery.

The legislative session was suspended for nearly an hour; then the speaker announced that the press is free in the chamber. Ms. Khabab was not ejected from the meeting.

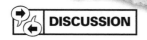 **DISCUSSION**

How big a deal is modesty in our culture these days? Has it gone the way of the horse and buggy, or do you see signs of modesty today?

Turn to a neighbor and weigh in on the issue. Discuss this:

• **Is our culture modest? What would you like to see changed—if anything?**

You'll have about two minutes to talk.

Go.

SOURCE: Reuters, "Woman in Jeans Causes Uproar in Parliament"

And You Think *Your* Wallet Is Thick

TOPIC: Money
SCRIPTURE: Hebrews 13:5

It's a fact: Many North Americans have a problem with credit cards. North Americans have too many cards and use them far too often.

But if you think you have a lot of credit cards, consider Walter Cavanagh.

At last count, Cavanagh owns 1,497 credit cards—all valid, by the way—which give him access to more than $1.7 million in credit.

POWERPOINT SHOW: Money 1

It started as a bet between Walter and a friend in 1969 to see who could collect the most cards in a year. Walter snagged 143 and won the bet—and the prize of a dinner—and then Walter just kept going.

By the way, he *also* has the world's largest wallet.

WRITING

In the U.S. several major credit-reporting agencies keep score of how well you and I manage credit.

But there's a smaller agency that matters, too. It's you.

In the space provided for you in the bulletin [or on the card you received when you entered], I'm going to ask you to jot a number between 1 and 10.

A "1" indicates that you have no problems with credit. In fact, you don't have any credit card debt that gets carried over from month to month. A "10" indicates that you think you're in terrible shape—you lose sleep and are often worried about credit card debt.

No one will see what you write unless you choose to share the number with others. Take a moment to jot your number down now.

SOURCE: The Associated Press, "Calif. Man Has 1,497 Valid Credit Cards"

Eager Beavers Claim Cash

TOPIC: Money
SCRIPTURE: Luke 12:16-21

When nearly $70,000 in cash disappeared from the Lucky Dollar Casino in Greensburg, Louisiana, officials had two immediate questions.

First, who took the money? The answer was allegedly a casino security guard who disabled security cameras and removed three bags of bills.

And the second question: Where had the cash been stashed?

After police were told the bags had been tossed into a creek, they found one waterlogged bag immediately. After some searching, the second bag was discovered where it had washed downstream and come to rest next to a beaver dam.

But what had happened to the *third* bag?

To better search deeper water, law enforcement officers began dismantling the beaver dam. That's when they found many of the remaining bills.

Beavers had torn open the bag and used bills as construction material. Greenbacks were woven in among sticks and brush to fill tiny gaps.

A substantial sum of cash was recovered, and no beavers were arrested.

POWERPOINT SHOW:
Money 2

SOURCE: The Associated Press, "Beavers Weave Stolen Cash Into Dam"

 **INTERVIEW**

Before your meeting, ask three people to serve on a panel that will respond after you tell a story. Don't tell the panel members what the story will be; just tell them they'll be asked to give a brief, off-the-cuff answer to a question.

Seat panel members in chairs where the congregation can see them.

After you've told the news story, set up the panel discussion by saying:

Actually, those beavers were pretty conservative with their money. They immediately put it into real estate and used it to make improvements.

How would people handle a sudden influx of cash? I've asked a panel of financial experts to tell us what they'd do with a bag of cash if one showed up outside their houses.

Expert one, what would you do?

Expert two?

Expert three?

Sons May Not Be Worth the Effort

TOPIC: Mothers
SCRIPTURE: Proverbs 23:24-25

POWERPOINT SHOW: Mothers

What follows will come as no surprise to any mothers in the congregation who are raising boys: Having a son may well shorten your life.

And I mean that *literally*.

Samuli Helle, a researcher at Finland's University of Turku, has co-authored a study based on his team's review of church records dated between 1640 and 1870.

Helle studied birth, death, and family records of Finnish women who bore children and reached at least 50 years of age. Granted, women living 200 or 300 years ago didn't have access to much institutionalized health care.

But everything else being equal, it appears that—at least for the Finnish mothers studied—the birth of each son shortened the mother's life by an average of 34 weeks.

That's 34 weeks *per son*.

One son: die 34 weeks early.

Two sons: die more than a *year* early.

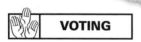 **VOTING**

What mothers here have sons? Raise your hands.

Two sons? Raise *your* hands…

Three or more sons? Raise *your* hands…

God bless—and save—you all.

Helle won't generalize the findings and doesn't claim the same statistics hold true today, but most mothers here have their own suspicions.

SOURCE: The Associated Press, "Study: Sons May Shorten Life Span of Their Mothers" by Paul Recer

Wild Goose a Dead Duck

TOPIC: Nature
SCRIPTURE: Romans 1:18-20

Kerry flew some 3,000 miles from Northern Ireland to the Canadian Arctic—then stopped cold. At least that's what satellites tracking the light-bellied Brent goose reported.

Kerry was one of six geese being studied and tracked by the National Geographic Society and Britain's Wildfowl and Wetlands Trust. What confused scientists was the bird's stop after such a long migration.

POWERPOINT SHOW: Nature

The transmitter attached to Kerry was still sending a signal—but not moving.

A search of wetlands near Canada's Resolute Bay didn't turn up the bird where scientists expected to find it—*in* the wetlands. But from that spot it was easy to zero in on Kerry's transmitter, which was in a nearby town…in a house…in a hunter's freezer.

That's right: Kerry the wild goose was one dead duck.

 **DISCUSSION**

Nature isn't always kind…especially over a duck blind. But nature *does* reflect the power and glory of its Creator.

What part of nature causes you to catch your breath and admire its beauty? A sunset over the ocean? A crisp, fall morning when frost paints your window?

Turn to someone sitting near you, and, in a few sentences, tell that person what part of nature prompts you to whisper, "Good job, God."

SOURCE: The Associated Press, "Wild Goose Chase Leads to Hunter's Freezer"

Oh-Oh in the OR

TOPIC: Pain
SCRIPTURE: John 16:20-22

For an Austrian woman, it already wasn't her best day.

She'd been admitted to a hospital.

For surgery.

For *abdominal* surgery, the kind of extensive procedure that requires a full surgical team and anesthesia.

At first the operation went well. The woman received a muscle relaxant, and the team went to work, preparing the machinery to keep the anesthetic coming as the surgery began.

It wasn't until another doctor entered the room and noticed that tears were forming in the eyes of the patient that someone checked the machine that was supposedly keeping the woman unconscious. Nobody had remembered to hook it up.

The muscle relaxant had paralyzed the patient and kept her from calling out or moving. But she wasn't receiving anesthetic. For 45 minutes the woman

had endured the surgical procedure—without pain-killers.

She'd felt it all.

The woman is, by the way, suing the hospital for nearly $80,000.

POWERPOINT SHOW:
Pain

SOURCE: Reuters, "Blunder Leaves Woman Awake for Surgery"

 **DISCUSSION**

Pain is something most of us avoid at any cost. In a world of painkillers, we see no reason that pain should be a part of our daily life.

But in reality, pain is a way of letting us know something is wrong. If you're a 50-year-old man and you feel a tightness in your chest and pain radiating down your left arm, the exact wrong thing to do is dull the pain—it's a messenger, and you need to hear it. Ignore it now, and you'll pay for the decision later.

That's true of most pain: It's trying to tell us something whether we experience it physically, emotionally, or spiritually.

Turn to someone sitting near you and discuss this question:

• **When was pain sending you a message you needed to hear?**

Canadian Jackpot Winner a Patient Man

TOPIC: Patience
SCRIPTURE: Proverbs 15:18

POWERPOINT SHOW: Patience

If you knew you could go pick up $23 million, how long would it take you to stop by the bank to get your check?

Raymond Sobeski took just under a year—12 days under, to be exact. Then he took his winning lottery ticket to the Ontario Gaming and Lottery Corporation to redeem his prize.

Sobeski is 47 years old and repairs computers. He knew almost immediately he was holding the winning ticket, but he wanted to take his time to sort through his options and decide what he'd do with the money.

The Canadian gaming organization was less patient. Knowing the winning ticket was out there somewhere, they purchased full-page ads in southwestern Ontario where the winning ticket had been sold.

But there was no danger of the ticket being unclaimed.

It was simply in the hands of a man who has been called the most patient man in Canada.

 **VOTING**

OK, let's be truthful: If you had a $23 million jackpot waiting for you to claim it, how long would you take?

How many of you would take a year? Raise your hands.

Six months?

One month?

Before lunch?

I've got to admit: I'd be awfully impatient to get that check in my hands, and I suspect most of you would be short on patience, too.

SOURCE: Reuters, "Patient Winner Waits a Year to Claim $23 Million"

Stealth Remote Promotes Silence

TOPIC: Peace
SCRIPTURE: Matthew 5:9

Just call Mitch Altman the peacemaker.

At least you can call him that if you're annoyed by a blaring television when sitting in a restaurant or hospital waiting room.

The San Francisco inventor is marketing "TV-B-Gone," a key chain that features an infrared remote control designed to turn off—and on—nearly 1,000 types of televisions.

POWERPOINT SHOW: Peace

Is that television blaring in the hotel breakfast room aggravating you? Quietly turn it off without anyone knowing you're the one who did it.

Are those 26 TVs in the sports bar a bore? Turn them off—at your own risk, of course.

After all, one person's peace is another person's missed playoff game.

 **INTERVIEW**

Television isn't the only thing that disturbs the peace in our lives. What about those heavy-footed neighbors who live in the apartment upstairs? Or the brain-bending thump-thump-thump of a car that's carrying a bass speaker the size of most Volkswagens?

What does it for you? Here's your chance to call out your pet peeve.

Look at the congregation, and encourage people to shout out the things that interrupt their peace. Be sure to repeat into your microphone what people say so everyone can hear the comments.

SOURCE: Fox News Network, LLC, "The 'Key' to TV Overload"

Christian Suffers in Hate Crime

TOPIC: Persecution
SCRIPTURE: Matthew 5:10

According to The Post-Crescent newspaper, the state of Wisconsin averages about 50 reported hate crimes per year. A hate crime includes criminal incidents motivated by race, religion, sexual orientation, and ethnicity.

In what's believed to be the first case on record in Wisconsin, a *Christian* has been targeted in a hate crime.

The victim had placed a sign in his yard that read, "You think you got it all? Got Jesus?" Three Wisconsin teenagers knocked on the man's door early in the morning, and when the victim answered, the teenagers pepper-sprayed him in the face.

According to a police complaint, the oldest of the teenagers was tired of Christian religious talk and of how his parents had raised him. Also, he expected the victim to be forgiving of the attack because of religious beliefs.

One of the teenagers, Sam Chartier, 17, was convicted of being a party to the use of mace in a hate crime and placed on two years' probation and

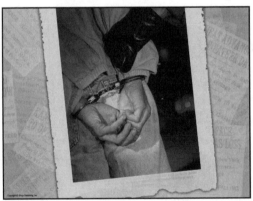

sentenced to 15 days in jail. Seven of those days were suspended when Chartier agreed to publicly wear a sign for five hours that read, "I'm convicted of a hate crime against a Christian."

POWERPOINT SHOW:
Persecution

SOURCE: The Post-Crescent, "Hate Crime Against Christian a First" by Dan Wilson

 **ACTIVITY**

There are Christians who suffer daily for their faith—but that isn't what most of us experience.

Here, we're often able to practice our faith without conflict. Here, we're safe. Our faith doesn't raise eyebrows, prompt police visits, or land us in jail.

In a few moments, I'm going to ask you to find a partner and together pray for Christians who are in dangerous surroundings, Christians who are paying for their faithfulness with their very blood and bones.

Ready? Find a partner, and let's pray for our brothers and sisters who are in danger.

If at First
You Don't Succeed...

TOPIC: Perseverance
SCRIPTURE: Hebrews 10:36

POWERPOINT SHOW: Perseverance

Harold Cohen is a patient man. He knows how to wait his turn.

He also knows how to *persevere*, as his college classmates at Brown University discovered.

At 84, Harold Cohen has completed a degree he'd intended to start when he was accepted at Brown in 1933. The sudden death of his father forced Cohen to shelve his plans for a college education until later.

"Later" turned out to be 50 *years* later when Cohen enrolled as a history major. That's the "patience" part of this story.

The perseverance comes into play when you consider *how* Cohen completed his education: one class per semester. It took Cohen 14 years to earn his bachelor's degree.

No word yet on his plans for graduate school.

 **INTERVIEW**

Before the service, ask several of your elderly church members if they're willing to be interviewed about times they've persevered in their lives.

Contact your interview subjects to confirm they'll be in attendance and to confirm that they can share their stories quickly and conversationally.

SOURCE: The Associated Press, "A Real Senior on Campus"

Plus, He Can't Get Life Insurance

TOPIC: Persistence
SCRIPTURE: 1 Corinthians 15:58

Finding a job these days takes persistence. But there are a few obstacles that no amount of persistence will help job seekers overcome.

Like being dead, for instance.

That's what Brazilian Marcio Freitas da Silva has discovered.

An unemployed driver, da Silva isn't unemployed by choice. A government paperwork problem has pretty much

POWERPOINT SHOW: Persistence

kept him jobless no matter how many applications he's filled out.

Three years ago, a man who shared da Silva's name died. Unfortunately, someone in the coroner's office listed da Silva's parents as the parents of the deceased man.

And since da Silva's parents have a son named Marcio who's officially considered deceased, that makes Marcio da Silva officially dead. Also unemployable, since dead people aren't allowed to drive and da Silva is a driver.

Not that da Silva has stopped *trying* to land a job. He's given it his best, but at this point his persistence is getting him nowhere until the rules change.

Which is also a problem. Marcio da Silva can't try to elect more sympathetic government officials.

In Brazil, dead men can't vote.

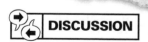 **DISCUSSION**

No question about it: da Silva is persistent...but how persistent are *you*?

In a moment I'm going to ask you to turn to someone sitting near you and tell about a time you stuck with something even though it seemed you couldn't accomplish it.

Ready? Each of you will have about one minute to tell about a time *you* were persistent. Go.

SOURCE: Reuters, "Can't Have a Job if You're Dead, Man Told"

India Reconsiders Moon Shot

TOPIC: Perspective
SCRIPTURE: 1 Corinthians 13:11-12

The Indian Space Research Organisation, India's version of NASA, is reconsidering a decision to place a man on the moon by the year 2015.

The problem isn't technology. India can develop the capacity to put boots on the moon's surface.

It's not necessarily an issue of cost, either, though a manned mission will likely take up to 10 years and cost a minimum of 100 billion rupees.

The problem is that, after thinking it over, the Indian government simply can't think of a good enough reason to put an Indian on the moon.

There's prestige, but the United States did it in 1969, so India can't get there first.

There are experiments that could be performed, but most of them can be done by remote control from Bombay.

When Indian scientists paused, pondered, and considered the goal from a broader perspective, it just didn't add up. The cost and risk far outweighed the return. In a country where poverty plagues a significant portion of the population, the rupees can be better spent elsewhere.

So don't expect the flag of India to be waving over the lunar surface anytime soon.

But *do* expect to see a few people who appear better fed.

POWERPOINT SHOW:
Perspective

SOURCE: Daily Times, "India Rethinking Its Plan to Send a Man to the Moon"

WRITING

Sometimes we think that just because we *can* do something, we *should* do it. Finance that new car, for instance, or take that promotion at work.

We get swept away with the possibilities and lose perspective.

On the blank space in your bulletin [or on the card you received when you entered], write these words: "Whatever you say, Lord."

Why those words? Because "whatever you say, Lord" reflects our ultimate perspective on options we consider, questions we answer, and decisions we make. Whatever else is involved, we're first and foremost servants of God.

Whatever you say, Lord.

Lawmakers Launch Lunches

TOPIC: Politics
SCRIPTURE: Daniel 6:4

POWERPOINT SHOW: Politics

Some people might consider it an improvement.

During the 1980s and 1990s, legislators in Taiwan occasionally got involved in fistfights during heated debates. The legislators have also been known to toss paper at each other.

But all that history faded into the background when angry lawmakers got into an old-fashioned food fight during a committee luncheon. Takeout box lunches loaded with rice, vegetables, meat, and hard-boiled eggs were launched as a debate raged concerning Taiwan's purchase of United States military material.

As much as the United States might wish to sell several billion dollars of weapons to Taiwan, caution is advised. Do we really want missiles in the hands of politicians who can't resist launching lunches?

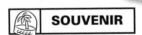

SOUVENIR

Before your congregation arrives, place an individually wrapped piece of chocolate on each seat.

As you sat down today, you may have noticed a piece of chocolate. I placed it there so if you decide to start a food fight with me, you'll be tossing *chocolate* my direction...not rice and hard-boiled eggs.

Some of you might keep the chocolate as a reminder of today's service. But I'm willing to bet you'll just eat it, which is what I intend to do with my piece right now. Join me.

When lawmakers get involved in food fights, you might wonder if the right people were elected. And you can certainly say that, especially after a food fight, politics can be a dirty business.

SOURCE: Canoe, "Food Fight in Taiwan's Legislature"

Think What It Would Have Cost for a Chin, Too

TOPIC: Popularity
SCRIPTURE: 2 Samuel 15:5-6

If you're seen and beloved by millions, but you don't know it, does that count as popularity?

Maybe not, but it can certainly be profitable.

Russell Christoff is a former model and actor who's now a kindergarten teacher in the San Francisco Bay Area. Back in 1986, he posed with a cup of Taster's Choice coffee and was paid

POWERPOINT SHOW: Popularity

$250 for the photo shoot. It wasn't a great deal of money, but Christoff was promised an additional $2,000 if his image appeared on the Canadian version of the Taster's Choice label.

Christoff never heard back, but 16 years later he noticed a familiar face looking back at him from the Taster's Choice label...*his* face, shown from his mouth up.

Used without permission...in 18 countries...for up to six years.

Nestle USA offered Christoff $100,000 to settle a lawsuit for using the model's likeness without permission, but Christoff turned the company down. Likewise, Nestle USA turned down Christoff's request for $8.5 million.

A Los Angeles County Superior Court jury set the settlement at $15.6 million—a decision almost certain to be appealed.

WRITING

What's something that most celebrities do on a regular basis?

That's right—sign autographs!

Using the blank space in your bulletin [or the card you received when you entered], sign your autograph. Sign it with a flourish, as if a fan were waiting to snatch it away and treasure it forever.

How did that feel? Awkward? Imagine if you were so popular that signing autographs was part of your routine!

SOURCE: The Associated Press, "Model Gets $15.6 Million Award From Nestle"

Porn Useful

TOPIC: Pornography
SCRIPTURE: Colossians 3:5

POWERPOINT SHOW: Pornography

To Doug Eichelberger, pornography isn't *completely* worthless.

He can always use it to build a barn.

The Colorado architect has used 80 tons of adult magazines, which can't easily be recycled because of their laminated pages, to frame a horse barn on his property.

The magazines sit on a foundation made of compressed pop bottles, milk jugs, and other "trash."

The porn-trash combo makes for a useful structure. It's well insulated, can handle the Colorado weather, and doesn't attract rats.

What more could Eichelberger ask for?

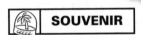 **SOUVENIR**

Before people arrive, place a metal washer on each seat. Hold up a washer as you continue talking.

When you came in, you found one of these washers on your seat. I put it there because it's the sort of washer I've seen used at construction sites. It's a solid building material.

I give it to you as a reminder that some things are more useful than others when you're building to last, when you want a firm foundation.

Eichelberger found a use for some 80 *tons* of pornography. But in your life, building on pornography is a tragic mistake. It doesn't provide a firm foundation in any way.

SOURCE: The Denver Post, "Waste-Watching Architect Raises Barns, Awareness"

What's a Decimal Point Between Friends?

TOPIC: Poverty
SCRIPTURE: Proverbs 14:23

When Japan's finance minister, Masajuro Shiokawa, spoke at an Asian Development Bank meeting in Shanghai, the delegates paid careful attention.

After all, Japan is an economic powerhouse in the region. Any donation by Japan toward reducing poverty would be both helpful and likely substantial.

And it was. *Very* substantial.

Speaking in Japanese, Shiokawa said

POWERPOINT SHOW: Poverty

Tokyo was ready to donate $500 billion to the Japan Fund for Poverty Reduction at the bank. The representatives from poorer nations were still reeling from the good news when a transcript of the speech made it clear that Shiokawa had misspoken.

The amount wasn't 500 *billion*…it was 50 *million*.

While $50 million is nothing to sneeze at, that figure is *considerably* less than initially promised.

 **DISCUSSION**

Let's pretend that a rich uncle has died and left you $50 million.

- **What would you do with that money to help relieve poverty? Anything? If something, what?**

Turn to someone seated next to you, and share what you'd do.

After several minutes draw attention back to yourself, and then continue.

Now let's assume that you don't have that rich uncle. You don't have an extra $50 lying around. What can you do with the resources you already have to help that plan or those programs anyway? Are you willing to move past realizing what you can't accomplish with limited resources to let God use you to do what you *can* accomplish? Carry that question home with you today.

SOURCE: Reuters, "$500 Billion Donation With Slip of the Tongue"

God Answers Prayers, Not Necessarily Mail

TOPIC: Prayer
SCRIPTURE: Matthew 6:5-6

POWERPOINT SHOW: Prayer

When people decide to send a letter to God or Jesus Christ, where do those messages go?

Some are destroyed. Some probably end up in a drawer in a local post office.

But others—thousands of them—are forwarded to Jerusalem. For years, letters from around the globe have made their way to the Postal Authority's center for undeliverable mail.

Some of the letters are opened, read, and sent to the Western Wall—a traditional place of prayer.

According to postal spokesman Yitzhak Rabihiya, the writers of these letters are concerned with everything from health problems to homework assignments. Nothing seems too big or too small to be jotted down, addressed to God, and dropped in a post box.

 **ACTIVITY**

The good news for us is that we can talk to God and save the postage. And it's true: Nothing is too big or too small to take to God.

Let's take a few moments to actually pray together. In a minute I'll ask you to find someone seated near you to pray with. You can pray in a pair or team up with several people; it's up to you.

But do this: Once you've found a partner or two, *please* briefly share a prayer concern—something you'd like to bring to God. Then pray for your partner.

SOURCE: The Associated Press, "Letters to God End Up at Jerusalem Post Office"

Pride Goeth Before a Big Check

TOPIC: Pride
SCRIPTURE: Proverbs 16:18

The idea was to raise money for St. Catherine's school in Toorak, Melbourne, Australia. That's why the school's kindergarten class painted a small acrylic on canvas that was put up for auction at a school fundraising event.

POWERPOINT SHOW: Pride

And boy, did it ever perform.

When two wealthy parents both decided the painting would come home with them, a bidding war broke out...and quickly escalated.

Millionaire John Ilhan offered several hundred dollars, generous given that the young artists had created a painting that contained animals, kids, and a flower—maybe. Nobody could quite tell.

But another parent allegedly wished to prove that she could outbid Ilhan. She proved her point when Ilhan eventually abandoned the bidding war and her bid was declared the winner.

The winning bid? A cool $75,000.

The winning parent—who did pay the money—has since removed her children from the school and allegedly returned the painting to St. Catherine's.

 **ACTIVITY**

You'll notice that there's a blank spot in your bulletin [or on the card you received when you entered]. That's so you can take 30 seconds right now to create a drawing, one of which you're proud. Find a pen or pencil, and create your masterpiece. Ready? Go.

After 30 seconds have passed, continue.

Now, any of you who thinks you've created artwork worth $75,000, *please* give it to me after our time together today. I want to get it up on eBay as soon as possible!

SOURCE: News Limited, "Kinder Painting Sold for $75,000" by Jeremy Calvert

Lost Couple Finally Located

TOPIC: Purpose
SCRIPTURE: Acts 20:23-24

POWERPOINT SHOW: Purpose

It's easy to confuse action with accomplishment and progress with purpose. Busy people *look* as if they're getting things done and moving ahead—but it's not always true.

Consider this story that's filled with forward motion—but not much purpose.

William and Violet Kaczmark, both in their 80s, set out on a drive to a family event scheduled at Harrah's Casino near St. Louis. They got in their car in suburban Florissant, Missouri, for what should have been a fairly quick trip south to Maryland Heights.

The problem was that they got lost. Not just a little lost, mind you. They got driving-through-the-night, not-a-*clue*-how-to-get-home lost. Violet suggested they ask for directions, but William refused.

So they just kept driving. All night. Nearly 24 hours straight.

The couple racked up the miles—they stopped for gas three times—but by the time the family called the police to report the couple missing, the family function was over. There was no longer any purpose in the Kaczmarks' trip.

A local media alert tipped off another motorist who spotted their car and convinced the Kaczmarks to pull over and wait for police.

The Kaczmarks made it home safely.

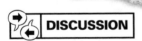 **DISCUSSION**

We've all found ourselves zooming along, making great time, but not actually accomplishing much.

Turn to someone sitting next to you, and tell about a time that happened to *you*. And if that person happens to be your spouse, who also refused to stop for directions, be kind.

SOURCE: KSDK.com, St. Louis, "Missing Florissant Couple Drives for Hours" by Rebecca Wu

Officer Gets Unexpected Award

TOPIC: Repentance
SCRIPTURE: 2 Corinthians 7:10

As an Illinois State Trooper, Lonnie Murbarger has sent his share of drunk drivers to court—or to jail.

So it's no surprise that very few have checked back later to say, "Thanks."

After 12 years in law enforcement, Murbarger experienced a first when Tasha French not only thanked him for arresting her, but also awarded him with a plaque for saving her life.

POWERPOINT SHOW: Repentance 1

French hadn't been so thankful three years earlier when she was pulled over, but her experience with the DUI arrest changed her life. She's now not only attending Alcoholics Anonymous, but she's also telling about her struggle in area prisons to help those who are battling alcohol and drug dependency.

 **WRITING**

French understands repentance because she's lived it. She's turned from one direction to the exact opposite one.

Real repentance requires not just avoiding some behavior, but embracing other behavior. Someone who's repented of eating poorly doesn't just stop eating; that person starts eating in a healthy way. Someone who repents of abusing a drug doesn't just stop doing drugs; that person substitutes healthy behavior.

Using the space provided in the bulletin [or on the card you were given as you entered], write yourself a note.

First identify something you need to repent. It can be anything; nobody will see this paper unless you choose to share it. Then write the new behavior you think should take the place of the sinful or harmful activity you're repenting.

SOURCE: Evansville Courier & Press, "Thanks, Busted Drunken Driver Tells Trooper" by Len Wells

Pickup Tragedy in Minnesota

TOPIC: Repentance
SCRIPTURE: Acts 3:19

POWERPOINT SHOW: Repentance 2

When Christopher Bergerson's pickup truck swerved off of County Road 11 west of Mankato, Minnesota, he wasn't wearing a seatbelt.

The truck hurtled nearly 150 feet over Highway 68, collided with a barrier, and then careened another 40 feet before catapulting over a fence. Bergerson's truck then rolled more than 100 feet before smashing into a tree.

The driver, who didn't survive the accident, was pinned beneath the truck when it then caught fire.

Investigating officers noted the following two facts in their reports:

First, Bergerson was ejected from the truck because he wasn't wearing a seatbelt.

And second, about 10 feet from the truck, they found a traffic ticket in the dirt. The ticket had been issued to Bergerson nine days earlier—for operating a vehicle without wearing a seatbelt.

WRITING

Repentance is about turning from one course of action and embracing another. It's about change—change for the better. When we won't make those changes, there's a price to be paid.

Using the blank space in your bulletin [or the card you received earlier], take 60 seconds to write down one change you need to make in your own life. Maybe it's as simple as forming the habit of belting up when you drive. Or maybe it's as challenging as changing your diet or your habit of speaking about others.

Nobody else will see your card, but I encourage you to take it home and let it be a prayer prompt for you this week.

There's room for repentance in all of our lives. Where's there room for repentance in yours?

SOURCE: The Associated Press, "Man Who Died When Thrown From Truck Had Been Ticketed for Not Wearing Seat Belt"

Naples Names New Top Pizza Maker

TOPIC: Reputation
SCRIPTURE: Proverbs 22:1

Think of it as the Super Bowl of pizza prowess.

The annual Naples pizza festival is where the best of the best of Naples' pizza chefs compete to create the perfect pizza pie—one worthy of being crowned "best" in a town where some say pizza was invented.

POWERPOINT SHOW: Reputation

And after the last slices had sizzled and the last toppings had been sampled, a new primo pizza-maker emerged: Makoto Onishi.

That's right: The best Italian pizza chef in Naples is Japanese.

Onishi went to Italy to study pizza making in Naples, and he must have learned well. Two years after arriving in Naples, he won the prestigious prize—and the reputation that came with it.

 **DISCUSSION**

Onishi got his reputation as Naples' top pizza maker by earning it—and that's what we all do to get our reputations.

Sometimes we earn our reputations by things we do...and other times by things we *don't* do.

Turn to a person sitting near you, and discuss your answer to this question:

• **If you could have any reputation, what reputation would you want?**

SOURCE: Australian Broadcasting Corporation, "Japanese Cook Named Best Pizza Maker in Naples"

But Does He Have to Clean Up Afterward?

TOPIC: Respect
SCRIPTURE: Romans 13:7

POWERPOINT SHOW: Respect

There's respect you get because of position, and there's respect you earn.

I want to talk about the second kind—the kind George Smith gets at Fern Ridge High School in Missouri's Parkway School District.

The seniors at Fern Ridge selected George Smith to be the speaker at their graduation ceremony because they consider Smith to be a role model. And because Smith has influenced their lives.

Smith accepted the honor.

After all, how often is a school custodian asked to speak at his school's graduation ceremony?

That's right: Smith isn't a sports star or a music idol whom kids have admired from afar. He's a janitor—someone they see day after day, close up. Someone who serves them and whose example has shaped them.

Along the way, the seniors at Fern Ridge have learned to respect George Smith.

Whether they also learned to pick up after themselves is unknown.

 **DISCUSSION**

George Smith has teenagers' respect—and he earned it the hard way.

In a moment I'm going to ask you to turn to someone sitting near you and tell about a person you respected when you were a teenager. Here's a question for you:

• **Who was it, and what did that person do to earn your respect?**

Ready? Find a friend and share that story. You'll have about one minute each.

SOURCE: St. Louis Post-Dispatch, "Fern Ridge High Students Pick Custodian to Be Graduation Speaker"

But Think What He's Saving on Insurance

TOPIC: Respect for the Law
SCRIPTURE: Romans 13:2

 VOTING

How many times would you have to be arrested—and sometimes jailed—for driving without a license before you finally gave up driving?

Would once do it for you? If so, raise your hand.

Twice? Anyone need to be arrested twice?

Three times?

POWERPOINT SHOW: Respect for the Law

For Raymond Morgan, a 24-year-old Australian, that number appears to be at least 31.

Morgan has been brought before the Redfern Local Court at least 30 times for driving without a license. He has been fined, had his license pulled, and even served 18 months in jail.

You'd think the message would have sunk in, especially since Morgan's license was pulled until the year 2999.

But apparently that wasn't enough.

Morgan has been arrested for driving again. The court extended the suspension until the year 3001, and in the interest of providing a more immediate consequence, magistrate Paul Falzon has sentenced Morgan to another six months in jail.

At least behind bars Morgan won't be able to climb behind the wheel.

SOURCE: News Limited, "Banned From Driving for Almost 1000 Yrs"

Man Misses Funeral

TOPIC: Resurrection
SCRIPTURE: John 11:25

Let's admit it: Some of us are in the habit of glancing through the obituaries in the paper.

Maybe it's because we want to know if one of our acquaintances has died. Or maybe it's for the satisfaction of not seeing our own names printed there.

But suppose for a moment that you *did* see your own name, right there in black and white.

What would you do then?

If you were Dane Squires, you'd pick up the phone and call the funeral home where your funeral was underway. And your call would arrive just as a body was being loaded into a hearse for a one-way trip to the crematorium.

When Squires' daughter was asked to take a call, the last person she expected to talk with was her father. *Literally* the last.

It seemed that Squires, living in Toronto, had been mistakenly identified as the victim of a commuter-train accident. Because he was a drifter, Squires hadn't been contacted to make certain the body's identification was accurate.

When he dropped in at his sister's house and the person who answered the door fainted dead away, Squires suspected *something* was up. When he saw the

obituary, he made a call and reached his daughter.

No word yet on whether the funeral home will give the Squires family a refund since they paid for a funeral Squires clearly didn't need.

POWERPOINT SHOW:
Resurrection

SOURCE: Fox News, "Man Telephones Own Funeral"

 **DISCUSSION**

Squires wasn't really resurrected—it just felt that way to his family.

There will come a day when Squires' funeral really *is* his funeral, and there won't be any phone calls for his daughter.

The odds are excellent that moment will come for all of us. We'll die…but those of us who know Jesus have reason to hope that we will be resurrected and will spend eternity with him.

In a moment I'm going to ask you to turn to someone sitting near you and discuss this question:

   • **How does it feel to know that resurrection has been promised by Some-
      one who has the power to deliver on that promise?**

Turn to a neighbor, and discuss this for a few minutes. How does it feel to know that resurrection has been promised by Jesus—who has the power to deliver on that promise?

Revenge *Is* Sweet

TOPIC: Revenge
SCRIPTURE: Leviticus 19:18

POWERPOINT SHOW: Revenge

There's an old saying that claims revenge is sweet, and a study released by the University of Zurich may support that notion.

The study was designed to allow subjects to get revenge if they thought they were being treated unfairly. And even though getting revenge cost the revenge-seekers money, most victims chose to even up the score.

The study used brain imaging to investigate what happened in the brains of people who chose to exact revenge.

Here's what the scientists found: Punishing people who've treated us unfairly fires up brain circuitry. And not just *any* circuitry; it fires up the region of the brain that registers pleasure and satisfaction.

The same portion of the brain, by the way, that fires up when people sniff cocaine.

Is revenge sweet? Not really…but taking revenge seems to help people feel better.

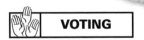 **VOTING**

Here's the question: Is feeling better a good enough reason to take revenge? Does that make taking revenge all right?

If we're honest, most of us have answered yes to that question at least once. We've taken revenge against someone who hurt us or who hurt someone we love.

If you've never taken revenge, please raise your hand.

Good for you. If I'd raised my hand, I'd have had to admit to a very faulty memory. It's human to take revenge—but it's not Christ-like.

SOURCE: ScoutNews, LLC, "Sweet Revenge May Be a Hard-Wired Reward"

In What Way Does This Explain James Bond?

TOPIC: Romance
SCRIPTURE: Isaiah 52:7

 VOTING

Men have long wondered exactly what attracts women, and a British survey has at last revealed the secret.

The survey, as reported on Australia's news.com Web site, says that…well, let's just do a quick survey of our own.

Ladies, how many of you believe that British women report that rock-hard pecs and chiseled muscles attract them? Raise your hands.

How many of you believe that a sparkling personality does the trick? Raise your hands.

How many of you think the British ladies interviewed said "shoes"?

Surprisingly—at least to me—that's what four out of five women surveyed said counted most when they're sizing up men and deciding if the guys are worthwhile. Over 66 percent of the women said that the style, color, and cleanliness of a man's shoes are significant indicators of what a man would be like in a relationship.

Apparently when it comes to romance, the sort of "soul" that matters most *isn't* the one that inspires poetry and flowers…it's the one on the bottom of a man's foot.

POWERPOINT SHOW: Romance

SOURCE: News Limited, "Shoes Made for Loving"

Saved in the Nick of Time

TOPIC: Salvation
SCRIPTURE: Ephesians 1:13

POWERPOINT SHOW: Salvation

A woman in Ridgeland, Mississippi, had a day that went from bad to worse to *really* worse. And it started with some lost keys.

The unidentified woman was searching *everywhere* for her lost keys. That apparently included checking the garbage bag she'd tossed in a Dumpster outside her apartment complex, because when the dump truck pulled up, the woman was right where she wasn't supposed to be: in the Dumpster.

The dump truck operator didn't realize the woman was in the Dumpster when he picked it up and emptied it. He didn't hear her yelling when he drove off, or during a two-mile drive.

Someone happened to hear shouting from inside the truck and alerted the driver. And that's a good thing—because the driver was in the process of crushing the garbage.

The woman was conscious when she was pulled out of the banana peels and coffee grinds and received medical treatment for aching joints.

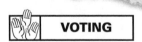 **VOTING**

How many of you have ever had a bad day? Raise your hands.

How about a day that was so bad you ended up being hauled away as garbage—or at least felt as if you had? Raise *your* hands.

Here's the thing: On bad days it's not enough to yell and scream and beat the side of the dump truck. We need to be rescued. We need a Savior, someone willing to launch a full-scale rescue operation.

And here's the good news: That's exactly what happened.

SOURCE: The Clarion-Ledger, "Woman in Dumpster Picked Up With Trash"

Rise...Shine...Thump

TOPIC: Self-Control
SCRIPTURE: Proverbs 25:28

Who here has teenagers? Raise your hand, and keep it up.

Who here regularly stays up past midnight? Raise your hand, too, please.

Now, who here thinks that getting up before 8:00 a.m. is cruel and unusual punishment?

All of you with your hands up will be happy to hear that Iris Klose, a 16-year-old girl in Germany, has solved the problem of rolling out of bed on time—literally.

POWERPOINT SHOW: Self-Control

It's called the "merciless bed." Once an alarm rings, the mattress rises 1 centimeter per minute. After five minutes the bed dumps the slow riser onto the floor.

 **WRITING**

Self-control requires...well, *self-control.* Rolling out of bed on time, not eating that extra cookie, remembering to exercise: all of these things take self-control.

And if you're like most people, there's at least some area of your life where self-control is in short supply.

In the blank area in your bulletin [or on the card you received when you came in], jot down one area of your life that could use more self-control. Nobody will see what you write unless you choose to share it.

SOURCE: Reuters, "Bed Forces Sleepyheads to Get Up"

Good Samaritans May or May Not Take Visa

TOPIC: Serving Others
SCRIPTURE: Galatians 5:13-14

POWERPOINT SHOW: Serving Others

Need the fire department in Fairfield, Iowa? No problem. Just call 911, and emergency personnel will be there in a heartbeat.

But expect a bill.

Following a vote by the city council, Fairfield residents can now expect to pay for services rendered. A vehicle fire will cost between $150 and $500; a house fire will range from $300 to $500; and if you're a business owner who finds your warehouse going up in flames, expect to pay between $300 and $1,000.

On a more personal note, if you're in an accident and you need to be extracted from a wrecked vehicle, the fee will be $500.

Fire Chief Ralph Hickenbottom notes that insurance companies will often pay the fees, so individual citizens won't pay out of pocket for the expense.

And reimbursed or not, the fire department is still serving others.

News reports didn't address whether the fire department takes credit cards.

 **ACTIVITY**

Let's practice serving others right now. In just a moment, I'm going to ask you all to stand up and find some way to serve another person in just 45 seconds. Maybe it will be giving someone a warm handshake and welcome. Maybe it's giving someone a great 20-second backrub. However you do it, serve someone else—and be open to being served by someone—in just 45 seconds.

Ready?

Go.

SOURCE: The Associated Press, "Iowa Fire Dept. to Charge for Services"

Pennies From Heaven

TOPIC: Stewardship
SCRIPTURE: Malachi 3:10

Suppose you're the priest of St. Joseph's Catholic Church and an elderly church member tells you he wants to donate his coin collection to the church.

What would you expect?

POWERPOINT SHOW: Stewardship

The Reverend Bob Hazel expected a few binders with carefully stored coins. Something to take to a coin shop or an online auction.

Except the donor, Melvin Doyle, wasn't exactly a collector in the sense that he traded a few rare coins. He was more of a "hang onto every coin that comes along" kind of collector. And he had been since 1918.

Doyle's stash of coins took three pick-up trucks to haul away.

True, there was a pretty good bunch of silver dollars and gold pieces, but there were also 1,340 pounds of pennies to sort through.

Doyle's donation promises to be somewhere in the $75,000 range once the rare coins are sold at auction and the rest are processed by a bank. The donation will be used to help remodel St. Joseph's.

 **SOUVENIR**

Here's what we don't know about Melvin Doyle: We don't know if he's a regular giver at St. Joseph's. We don't know if he tithes. All we know is that every 70 years or so he gives his loose change to the church.

And if that's *all* he does, that falls a bit short of what we'd normally call "stewardship."

Stewardship is using the resources God has given you to do his will and serve him. And here's the catch: *Everything* you have is a resource God has given you. It's all his.

When you arrived today, you received a shiny, new nickel. It's yours. It's a gift.

Here's my challenge to you: Be a good steward of the nickel. Use it as God directs you to use it…whatever that looks like.

SOURCE: Star Tribune, "New Hope Church's Plate Runneth Over"

Tough Day? Pass the Bonbons

TOPIC: Stress
SCRIPTURE: Numbers 6:25-26

POWERPOINT SHOW: Stress

When people are stressed out, they often eat. It's a way some of us relieve frustration.

But according to a study released in the Journal of Applied Social Psychology, when the cause of the stress has passed—when the kids are off to school or the annual review is over or you've been accepted into the college of your choice—some people frustrated by stressful situations *continue* to eat.

"Some people" as in *women*. And what's worse—those women tend to pick the worst possible treats to eat: snacks loaded with fat.

Forget low-fat pretzels, jelly beans, and popcorn. Stressed-out women in the study went straight for the cheese, white chocolate, and potato chips.

Lead researcher Laura Cousino Klein reports that women who were most frustrated during a 25-minute experiment tended to eat twice as much as women who weren't as frustrated.

The researchers blasted women with annoying sounds at 108 decibels—about the volume of a jackhammer—as the women completed a variety of tasks. In other words, it was a lot like daily life if you have kids in the house.

The researchers learned this: Just because stressful situations have passed doesn't mean we're back to normal. The impact can last awhile—and put pounds on our hips.

By the way, men who went through the experiment didn't change their snacking habits regardless of how frustrated they were.

Apparently men are either better able to handle stress…or they're clueless.

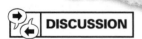 **DISCUSSION**

How do *you* handle stress? Maybe you resort to bonbons…maybe basketball. Find someone who's seated near you, and tell that person your answer to this question:

• **How do you handle stress?**

SOURCE: The Associated Press, "Loud Noise 'Prompts Women to Eat' "

Student Faces $10 Million Temptation

TOPIC: Temptation
SCRIPTURE: 1 Corinthians 10:13

Imagine this…

You're a freshman at Princeton University. Tuition is high, money is tight, and you could use a few bucks for a pizza.

While you're online checking the finances of the magazine for which you work, you notice that you've got the password that not only lets you find out how the magazine is doing but also gives you access to $9.9 million owned by Princeton University.

What do you do?

If you're Ira Leeds, you do nothing.

At least, nothing illegal.

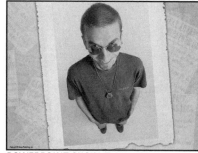

POWERPOINT SHOW: Temptation

Leeds, a Princeton University freshman, is the financial manager for The Princeton Tory, a University publication. He keeps track of how many stamps the magazine buys and how much has been spent on lunches and envelopes.

While checking the magazine's account online, he noticed that his account was linked to 14 other university accounts—and between them there was nearly $10 million at his fingertips.

Leeds actually *did* do something: He alerted the university president and the university provost, neither of whom was happy with their bank.

Steps, as they say, have been taken.

 **ACTIVITY**

Before you came into this room today, I placed a $10 bill on one of the seats. On the bill, I put a sticky note that said, "Please put this money in the offering plate." If you found the bill, please put it in the offering today when the plate comes by.

Tempted to keep the money?

Suppose it was a $10 *million* bill.

SOURCE: The Associated Press, "Banking Glitch Gives Student $9.9 Million"

No Thanks—I'm Driving

TOPIC: Trust
SCRIPTURE: Proverbs 3:5-6

POWERPOINT SHOW: Trust

A study published by the American Psychological Association has demonstrated the power of trusting a lie...at least as far as drinking alcohol is concerned.

The experiment, conducted by researchers Maryanne Garry and Seema Assefi, of Victoria University in New Zealand, formed 148 students into two groups.

The first group was served tonic water. The second group was served tonic water but told it was vodka and tonic.

Both groups then watched a series of slides depicting a crime and read a summary of the crime—a summary that contained intentionally misleading information.

Students who thought they were drinking vodka in their tonic water made poorer eyewitnesses than their counterparts. Some students who believed they were drinking vodka even exhibited signs of intoxication.

Trusting a lie changed the students' behavior. And perhaps convinced the students to be slower to trust researchers in the future!

 **INTERVIEW**

Before your meeting, recruit three members of your congregation to interview. Ask:

- **How do you feel when someone or something you trust lets you down?**

- **What's a physical object that you trusted but that let you down?**

Contact your interview subjects early to confirm they'll be in attendance and to share the questions you'll be asking.

SOURCE: BBC NEWS, " 'Fake Alcohol' Can Make You Tipsy"

Michelin Book Boomerangs

TOPIC: Truth
SCRIPTURE: John 8:32

The truth hurts…at least, it can hurt business.

Every year, thousands of tourists who visit Europe do so with a copy of the Michelin guide tucked into their pockets. It's the ultimate guide to fine dining throughout Europe, and for years it has enjoyed a great reputation…until 2005.

POWERPOINT SHOW: Truth

The *Michelin Benelux Red Guide 2005*—a reference guide for dining in Belgium, the Netherlands, and Luxembourg—has been pulled off bookshelves because of an embarrassing error.

A restaurant in Belgium that was lauded for excellent, reasonably priced food was never actually visited by one of the reviewers Michelin uses to provide restaurant rankings. Even worse, the restaurant didn't exist at the time the review was supposed to have taken place. The building in which the restaurant was to be housed was nothing but a construction site at the time.

To its credit, Michelin pulled all 50,000 books just three days after they went on sale.

For this company, a compromised reputation is a ruined business. Telling the truth is not just the right thing to do, it's the only thing—at any cost.

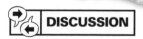 **DISCUSSION**

The truth sets you free—that's the promise in Scripture.

But first it can sometimes make you miserable because it forces you to take an open-eyed, honest look at yourself and your situation.

Turn to someone sitting near you, and share a time that hearing—or telling—the truth was tough for you. Maybe it was an evaluation you received at work or something a friend told you about yourself.

- **What was that time for you?**

SOURCE: Agence France-Presse, "Michelin Pulls Version of Famed Restaurant Guide After Overhasty Review"

Bomb Explodes— 60 Years Late

TOPIC: War
SCRIPTURE: Isaiah 2:3-5

POWERPOINT SHOW: War

The battle may be over, but the casualties keep coming.

In Okinawa, a Japanese construction worker was injured by shrapnel when a yellow-phosphorus bomb exploded at a building site. It's thought the bomb was dropped by U.S. forces during fierce fighting in the closing months of World War II.

The construction worker's injuries were superficial.

Discovering vintage bombs has happened before in Okinawa. Recently 5,000 Okinawans were temporarily evacuated from a residential neighborhood after another U.S. bomb was discovered nearby.

 **INTERVIEW**

Before your meeting, arrange to have three members of your congregation whose lives have been touched by war available for a panel interview. Ask the three people to sit facing the congregation, and let them know before your meeting what questions you'll ask.

After you tell the story, briefly introduce the panel, outline each member's relevant history, and ask the panel to respond to these questions:

- **In what ways did your exposure to war change you?**

- **If you had the power to erase wars from the future, would you? Why or why not?**

SOURCE: Reuters, "Man Injured After World War II Bomb Explodes"

Holy Rollers…Literally

TOPIC: Worship
SCRIPTURE: John 4:23-24

Worship matters. Involved, deep worship expressed in prayer, praise, or song has an impact on your life.

But did you know it can also have an impact on traffic?

That's what the Illinois state police discovered when several lanes of Interstate 94 were closed because of a bus rollover. The accident resulted in several significant injuries and more than 40 minor ones.

According to law enforcement officials, the bus was from Hyles-Anderson College, a school affiliated with the Baptist denomination. As they rode down the highway on that Saturday morning, passengers began to sway as they sang.

The passengers must have been swaying in unison, because their swaying literally tipped the bus over.

There's no official word as to what song prompted the accident, but you can bet it's been dropped from the College Travel Songbook.

POWERPOINT SHOW:
Worship

· · · · · · · · · · · · · ▶

SOURCE: NBC5.com, "Bus Rollover Closes Part of I-94"

 **ACTIVITY**

The worshippers on that bus learned a valuable lesson: Not every expression of worship is appropriate in every setting.

But I think it's great they were being expressive in worship, joining in corporate worship in a way that literally shook their world.

Here's a 30-second challenge for you: In a moment I'll ask that each of us move into a position that reflects how we worship best. I understand that perhaps that pose isn't the most appropriate in our corporate worship setting...but that doesn't mean it's wrong elsewhere in life.

We serve a God who didn't have a problem with David dancing in worship. If you worship God best by standing and raising your hands, kneeling, or even lying facedown on the floor—so be it. God bless you.

Or maybe you're a sit-quietly-with-head-bowed worshipper. Fine.

Let's take the next 30 seconds to move into our preferred worship positions. And let's celebrate the fact that the diverse ways we worship all reflect our love of God.

INDEXES

Scripture Index

Topical Index

Memory-Jogger Index

The Lord works in mysterious ways—and so does your memory. Here's a quick list of memory joggers to help you locate that specific story you *almost* remember.

EVALUATION FOR
News You Can Use

Please help Group Publishing, Inc., continue to provide innovative and useful resources for ministry. Please take a moment to fill out this evaluation and mail or fax it to us. Thanks!

Group Publishing, Inc.
Attention: Product Development
P.O. Box 481
Loveland, CO 80539
Fax: (970) 292-4370

• • •

1. As a whole, this book has been (circle one)
not very helpful   *very helpful*
1   2   3   4   5   6   7   8   9   10

2. The best things about this book:

3. Ways this book could be improved:

4. Things I will change because of this book:

5. Other books I'd like to see Group publish in the future:

6. Would you be interested in field-testing future Group products and giving us your feedback? If so, please fill in the information below:

Name_____

Church Name _____

Denomination _____ Church Size _____

Church Address _____

City _____ State _____ ZIP _____

Church Phone_____

E-mail _____